If I Can...

Anybody Can...

If I Can... Anybody Can
by Gary Shawkey with P.J. Russell

Gary Shawkey International, Inc
12468 Spring Hill Drive
Spring Hill, FL 34609
352-684-9216
http://www.garyshawkey.com

ISBN 0-970609-0-1

Contents

If I Can . . .
Anybody Can...

by Gary Shawkey with P.J. Russell

The incredible story of one man's struggle to succeed and what it takes to bring personal dreams into reality.

Dedication

This book is humbly and with reverence,
dedicated to those people in my life
who threw me the strong ropes when I was falling,
and offered me silver threads to cling to,
when hope was all I had.

And to those,
both known and unknown,
who gave me reasons for living.

First, to Stephanie
who came to me when I thought nothing like her was possible,
much less real, who brought such wonderful substance
and absolute joy and amazing love into my life.

To Teresa, who even in her suffering,
knew all along how it would all turn out.

To my four children,
Joey, Dawn, Heather and Jacob,
You are my reasons for being,
living testimonies that all things
are possible and wonderful
for those who finally manage to believe.

To my father, who by some major miracle
managed to survive my unholy existence and
to my mother who can finally rest in peace.

And to Gloria, dear Gloria
who gave me my life back,
and kept it from disappearing into a deep, dark hole
from which I would not have returned.
Who made it possible for me to
love and enjoy all the others
I have with me today
and to live through these wonderful years
I would surely have missed
had it not been for your blessed compassion,
unselfish love and unfaltering belief in
a sometimes thoughtless, always wild,
and often wayward boy
others thought worthless and without redeeming value.

They were wrong, Aunt Gloria,
and you,
bless your sweet heart,
were right all the time!

Introduction

When the idea for this book was first discussed, it was simply that I wanted to tell my story...like a lot of people do. Anyone who has a life, has a story to tell. A friend of mine convinced me there are no dull life stories, just dull story tellers, so I made it my business to try to find one who could "tell it like I lived it," and I believe I have done that. Because of my success (after years of failure after failure after disastrous failure) the book began to take on a motivational tone, still of course, with all the extremely personal undercurrents.

It occurred to me that if I could become a multi-millionaire before reaching the age of thirty-five, and if I could successfully manage an international corporation after sending numerous other projects, schemes and companies to an early grave, then maybe I had something worthwhile to share with others. I also knew that because of the incredible beginning of my somewhat jaded and often out-of-control life, followed by periods of pure devastation and utter hopelessness, I could certainly prove beyond a shadow of a doubt, that yes, it can be done. If, after all the adversities I had encountered, all the pain and disappointments I had survived, all the failures I had overcome, I could still show the reader that if someone with all those strikes against him could still emerge victorious...then I'm here to tell you—Anybody Can.

Anybody can go into business for themselves and make success happen if they follow a few simple rules. I've come to the conclusion that there are no "new stories," old untold "secrets" and certainly nothing new under the sun. Whether it is the success of Donald Trump, Don Lapre, Anthony Robbins, Martha Stewart or Oprah Winfrey, the formula is the same.

Know you can do it. And, just do it. It's that simple.

Robbins tells us to take immediate control of our mental, emotional, physical and financial destiny. Your first grade teacher or some wise old neighbor probably told you pretty much the same thing in so many words. It's quite simple and nobody has a patent or copyright on it. So, if you are expecting a new and innovative road map which will point the way (with numerous shortcuts) to riches and happiness, you might as well close the book and go back to flipping burgers at the fast food place down the street— something I've done, again and again.

Critics and fans both have likened Robbins to a present-day guru who offers all of us a better life if we simply apply sound principles and techniques, coupled with a self-awareness and the sincere belief that we can do whatever we set out to accomplish. Stephen Covey, author of "The 7 Habits of Highly Effective People" wrote that Robbins is one of the great influences of this generation, adding that "true success is first anchored to enduring values and service to others."

Robbins dedicated his book "Awaken the Giant Within" to the "unlimited power that lies sleeping within you. Let it slumber no more." Frederick L. Covan, PhD, the Chief Psychologist at Bellevue Hospital in New York wrote in the acknowledgments of the same book that "empowering people to realize that they can determine the outcome of their own lives is not always easy." He went on to say however, that it can be done, because Robbins and millions of others have done it repeatedly.

It is not my intent to try to put myself on the same level, or even in the same ballpark or parking lot with Anthony Robbins, but having applied his principles which are the same principles he embraces, the same ones used by Trump and almost all other successful people, to my own life, I know that it works. I am living proof and I know many others who can make the same claim.

Is it some deep mysterious secret?

No.

Is it some complicated formula?

No.

Is it easy?

Absolutely—possibly with some stops and starts.

Would I recommend it?

What do you think?

Tony Robbins has told us time and again, in his amazing seminars and best-selling books that we all have a special gift. I have always believed that, but having proved it with my own success and having watched others prove it in themselves, I am much more than just a believer now. I am one of the best examples I know, of a man who has been all the way down into the deepest despair life can dish out, and finally manage, through that inborn survival instinct to keep going, and finally, to triumph. When I tell you it can be done, the words are coming from one who has been there several times and done that again and again. I know that we can all have a vision for a better quality of life if we just tap into our unlimited power and watch it happen.

By now, you already know that I am a great admirer of some of the outstanding motivational people like Robbins who have come all the way from below bottom to make it to the top on sheer will power and hard work. Just as I have learned from others, I hope you can learn from me. When Tony Robbins said that "Success truly is the result of good judgment. Good judgment is the result of experience, and experience is often the result of bad judgment," I felt as though he'd been reading my mail. He was describing me, speaking to me, and I not only listened, I used the information to make my life better. I'm sure you will recognize yourself a time or two in these pages, and it is my fervent hope that you will derive some inspiration, motivation, comfort and/or pleasure from the information I am sharing with you.

It was also Robbins who told us that "The secret of success is learning how to use pain and pleasure instead of having pain and pleasure use you. If you do that, you are in control of your life and if you don't, life controls you." You will see in my book how I have gone through enormous pain and exquisite pleasures. I also subscribe to his notion that no matter how hard you work, even if you know everything there is to know, if you are heading east looking for that illusive sunset, you'll never get there.

Direction is the key word here. Direction is what it takes to get you from where you are—to where you want to be. You have to remember too, that direction can also take you from where you are—to where you really don't want to be, so your choice of direction is extremely critical.

This book itself is a solid recommendation about taking control of your own life and allowing your innate knowledge to guide you toward a better tomorrow in every phase and element. That sounds like a commercial for all the motivational speakers and self-improvement seminars (some of which are a lot of crap) but I promise you, that's not what it is. To quote an old TV detective on Dragnet, what I hope to offer you with these wild words of wisdom (hopefully) and revelations of the pain and pleasure of my own experiences are simply, "just the facts, Ma'am... or Sir..."

What I also want to accomplish is what I said in the beginning. I want you to realize that you can arrive at your destination in spite of yourself, as well as because of yourself. In my case, I took the long, rocky, rough way around. I did all the wrong things right, and all the right things wrong, but along the way I learned something. I learned that if you expect failure you won't be disappointed. If you expect to fall down, most likely you will. If you think you can't realize your dreams, they will for certain turn to nightmares. I don't know if somebody said this, or it is something which came from my own mind, but I believe if you expect to be disappointed, disappointment is exactly what you'll get.

In my younger years, I made life as hard on myself as I could most of the time. Other times I allowed life to take me on adventure after adventure as I ate up the scenery with gusto and all the passion I could muster. Being motivated or even successful was not foremost in my mind. Tomorrow wasn't even foremost in my mind most of the time. Getting through the day—and/or the night or even the next hour, was more on the level I operated. My recipe for life was so full of errors that I have to wonder at times how I ever muddled through some of my half-baked ideas. If you took all the wrong ingredients and mixed them up in all the wrong ways and baked them in the wrong oven at the wrong temperature, for the wrong amount of time, then you would have the recipe for my own personal cake of life in those very early days. What I want to make the reader understand is how I took all those negatives and still managed to turn them inside out, turn my life completely around , and come out a winner after all—then this book will have served its purpose.

If there were one single concept I could say to make it easier for you to get to where you want to be, who you want to become, or just take your life to the next level, it would have to be the single most important lesson I learned from the beginning. Get personal in whatever you are doing and be personal with whoever you are doing it with. Right now you have begun a journey with me.

You have made the commitment to at least read the first book in my "Anybody Can" series. Let's get personal my friend. My commitment to you is to tell you everything I have learned so far. A road map if you want to call it that. I also want to commit my services to all who purchased this book. Feel free to send me a message anytime at anybodycan@garyshawkey.com. But first, I have to tell you who I am and what it took to get where I am in the present day.

Looking back on the monumental undertaking of this book, I want to make it completely clear that this was certainly not a one-man show. Without the lights of my life, there would have been no illumination. Without the many props and background there would have been no stage setting. Without the words being placed in their proper order there would have been no text, script, or continuity. Without the production manager there would have no production. Without the director there would have been no direction. Without the hard work of all the supporting cast and crew who helped us get this piece of work together, it simply could not have happened. Without the extensive makeup, we would not have looked quite as good. Without the colorful costumes we would have all been naked.

As it is now, I'm the only damned fool out here in my all-togethers.

Prologue

If I could only make it to the door, I thought.

The distance from the middle of the room to the doorway seemed like a thousand miles and I honestly felt that each step I took might be my last. The constant pounding on the wall and the pitiful screams that filled the small seedy motel room seemed to extend far beyond any measurable sound as they roared like angry thunder inside my head, spreading out like poison tentacles throughout every part of my body.

I had to get out.

Once I stepped into the hot, sultry Georgia night, I drew a deep breath, only to discover that the very act of breathing made me even sicker. My illness wasn't physical however—that was poor Teresa's department. She was the one suffering pain that I could neither share nor stop. I had promised to take good care of her. I had given her my solemn oath that no matter what happened, I would continue to be that brave rescuer, that dashing Knight who had ridden in on a white horse and saved her from the low-down, red-necked Dragon seven years before.

Yeah well—some brave hero I turned out to be.

I was now helpless and worse yet, without hope of any kind. All the encouraging words I'd given her, all the up-and-at 'em speeches I'd made, all the times I'd solemnly assured her that

everything would be all right, that old Gary could fix anything; all
of it was lost in the agony of finally realizing that it was all over.

As I closed the door behind me, I leaned forward to rest my
head against the facing door, as though the simple crossing of a
room had sapped what little strength I had left. I could still hear
the terrible pounding of Teresa's head as she butted it against the
wall time and time again, trying to lessen the agony of her indescribable pain. That disturbing sound was punctuated by the cries
of my four-year old daughter, Dawn, all of which seeped through
the thin walls separating me from the two people who meant more
to me at the time than anyone else on earth.

For a long time, I stood like a zombie by the door of the cheap
dilapidated motel on the underbelly side of Atlanta.
"Is this what we've come to, Teresa," I half whispered. "Is this
the mansion I promised you? Where is the good life we planned
for? Is this it? Where's the money? Where are the damn good
times? Where is that golden promise of a great tomorrow?"

All gone.

Several ladies of the evening and drug pushers passed me with
only a suspicious or casual glance. I wasn't even considered worth
their efforts. I looked too much like the loser I had become. I
couldn't believe the month of June was so hot, but that was
Georgia for you. I could feel the bottom of the world closing over
me like a funeral shroud. The garish neon lights from the porno
shops and bars flashed off and on, almost in rhythm to the pounding and the screaming which was still coming from the room.

Quickly, I crossed the uneven sidewalk to the parking lot. I
honestly don't know if I considered getting in my car and driving
off the edge somewhere or not, but I knew I could not stay for one
more second within hearing distance of my wife and my daughter,

and next to the place where my whole world was falling into a million pieces on the stained carpet of a stifling twelve-by-twelve room.

"You are such a piece of crap, Gary" I angrily accused myself, and myself made no effort of defense. I had none. Fumbling for a cigarette then, I realized that my hands were shaking so violently I could hardly hold a match to get it lit.

"I'm sorry, Teresa... Oh dear God, I'm so sorry..."

I wanted to look upward again, to plead my case, and Teresa's, before God one more time, but I'd gone there so many times, sometimes receiving the answers I sought, then again, not. I was beginning to lose what little faith I had, and I couldn't help but wonder if I had any right to ask anything else of Him, since I'd done so little to earn any kind of mercy.

"For Teresa, God... help her," I begged. "...And for Dawn... please..."

I wanted to reach up and shake my fist at the sky in the hope of getting His attention, but I knew that would be futile as well as foolish.

"Darn you, Teresa..." I said then, once again taking out my pain on her. I blamed her because she would never take care of herself. She wouldn't take her shots. She wouldn't follow her diet. She wouldn't listen to the doctors when they warned her that she either walked the line they drew, or the line would run out. She cursed them and defied them at every opportunity. She seemed to be determined to live life her way, regardless of the consequences.

"Darn it, it's my life," she would say, and I would correct her by telling her it was my life too. Later, I reminded her it was the baby's life as well, but she seemed determined to thumb her nose at all the odds, and ride the wild pony until he fell over. To heck with the dialysis. To heck with the insulin shots. To heck with them all. She was captain of her own ship and she was going to sail it into whatever waters she chose, regardless of the black clouds and storm warnings.

Now, she was sinking fast. She knew, and I knew. Worst of all, Dawn knew.

I wished then I could just let loose and cry, but for some reason I was denied that release as well. So I stood, dry-eyed and powerless, in the almost empty parking lot and tried not to think about all the fine and grandiose plans that had gone down the drain, all the dreams we never got to live, and all the love we had promised to share forever. Now, even forever had come and gone and we were left with only the sad residue of burned bridges, broken dreams and roads not taken.

"I failed you, Teresa... and worse yet, I'm failing Dawn."

I could see Dawn's beautiful little face in front of me, a small replica of her mother's, with those big blue eyes and rosy cheeks framed by a mass of light brown hair. The wide smile and the childish laughter however, had long been replaced by a countenance of horrible dread and continuing terror, born of the childlike perception that she was in real danger of losing her mother to some unknown assailant. Even though the word "death" meant little to a four-year old, she had heard it, and she recognized all the signs of its ghastly approach.

"Poor baby..." I said aloud, as I smashed the half-smoked cigarette into the littered pavement. I didn't know if I was referring to Dawn or Teresa, or both of them.

Truth told, I could have even been referring to myself.

The First Chapter

The Incredible Beginning

"Adversity has the effect of eliciting talents,
which in prosperous circumstances would have lain
dormant."
—Horace

Even the occasion of my birth was touched by rather bizarre and certainly unconventional events. It was not until years later when I learned of the unusual circumstances of my beginnings that I began to wonder if it was some sort of omen or a strong indication that my life was not going to follow the yellow brick road into the land of Oz.

Or, maybe that's exactly what it did.

The Chinese have a saying that every child born is like a blank page, and each person who comes in contact with him or her, will write upon that page either words of wisdom or words of woe, sometimes both. Some will write many things while others may only put down a single word. Whatever is written on the page will, in turn, dictate the kind of person that child will become, offering values as well as strength and/or weakness of character.

Welcome to the world, Gary Shawkey. Here's your blank page.

I didn't dash for that front row seat in life's theater so I could observe what things were all about. Instead, I headed for the rides and the games, pushing ahead to fully experience all I could squeeze in, before the roller coaster made me puke or the Merry-go-round caused me to fall down dizzy on the ground.

Unbeknownst to me at the time of my birth, my parents had chosen to get their baby boy in a manner not totally on the up-and-up-which, now that I think of it, figures.

Because of their ages, my mother was in her 40s and my dad in his 50s, they were not exactly put at the head of the list as potential adoptive parents. They tried all the agencies and adoption services, but each time met with the same opposition and were told they were simply "too old" to adopt a baby. "Perhaps an older child." No, they wanted a little baby, a newborn if possible, very badly I was told. Many people who desperately want something may go out of their way to get it, bend the law if need be. In my case, they bent the heck out of it.

They bought me: Paid for me with good hard cash. The good old American way, and all that stuff. My dad laid down a cool thousand dollars in small bills and didn't even ask for a receipt. After all, he had me. What more could he need? Later I would of course, cost him many, many more thousands of dollars, so believe me, that first thousand was just a small down payment on this particular baby.

It all began, I found out later, when my mother had expressed her compelling need for a child to the Monsignor at St. Martha's Catholic Church on North Hill, an area where I would come to live and grow up. He gave her the name, or somehow put her in touch with a man she was told to be a fine old country doctor in Georgia who might be able to help them.

My potential parents called this Doctor Hicks and he offered them a deal they could not, and did not, want to refuse. They would agree to pay the amount of money he asked, and when he called them, they would have to be in McCaysville, Georgia in twenty-four hours.

They agreed.

On September 20, 1963, a loud speaker at the Indian's stadium in Cleveland boomed the page for Sigmund and Irene Shawkey. The labor pains had begun, and my parents left the baseball game before the third inning, drove home, threw their already packed suitcases in the car and headed south.

The baby was coming.

When they returned home, they presented me as the latest member of the Shawkey family.

"This is the baby we adopted. Isn't he darling?"

He was. I am darn sure of that.

I don't know what went through their minds as they drove the 1,400 plus miles round trip. They never talked about it with me, except to make it clear from the beginning that I was adopted. The sketchy details of the rest of the fabricated story of my beginnings was not exactly one of much imagination, however. I was told simply that my birth parents had both been killed in a tragic automobile accident. I had no reason to doubt the terrible tale, for it was the same one told to other members of my family, who in turn, related it to me time and again.

"Poor little Gary... had a bad start... losing both his Mommy and Daddy like that..."

"What started out as a tragedy has turned into something wonderful..."

Sounded all right to me, but I can't recall ever caring one way or another about my origin, or how it all came about. I was reasonably happy with the parents I had.

I had no idea that there would one day be national headlines, television talk shows and "projected movie deals" and more than a big hurrah all over the country about the circumstances of my birth and that of several other babies who were also placed on the open market by this "good doctor Hicks."

Talk about your "tangled web."

The man who had paid what he considered a fair price for me was a graphic artist for Firestone Tire and Rubber at the time, and his work, as I came to recognize later, was quite good. Dad was much valued by the company until his retirement. He also worked as a free-lance artist, and his paintings were featured in art shows and museums all around the country. Some of my earliest and most fond recollections were of traveling to various places with him, where his art was being shown and sold. My mother was also artistically bent, and was well known in the Akron area as one of the best floral arrangers around. She had a gift, they said. She was active in the garden clubs and from all appearances, little Gary had lucked into one near-perfect family. Successful father, kind and handsome. Wonderful mother, beautiful by any standard, with the tasteful May Company clothes and the chic beauty salon hair. Good home. Good strong Catholics. Upstanding citizens. Oh yeah, and then there was this terrific child, smart, cute and healthy. Made one doggone fine Christmas card photo.

Love, and a very Merry Christmas from Sig, Irene and Little Gary.

December, 1963.

There were, however, one or two little flaws in the negative.

The handsome, successful father, who was rather stiff-necked and stern, put in a lot of hours at his work both at Firestone Tire and Rubber Company and in his own art business. The perfectly groomed and artistic garden lady was an alcoholic.

To further muddy the waters, this seemingly perfect couple, who said all the correct things in public, had good manners and were presentable in any company, fought like alley cats and junk yard dogs behind closed doors.

The kid, the one who had been proudly purchased, could hear it all through the thickness of any door. I learned early to tune out the whole blamed mess. It wasn't a case of not believing I was loved. It was a case of wondering who in the heck these people were who claimed to love me.

My mother, when she wasn't sucking on the Wild Irish Rose bottle or stashing cheap ripple in the clothes basket, was a kind and loving person. When she was sober, she treated me extremely well and spent more a considerable amount of time supplying me with the proper amount of hugs and ample assurances of love. I must have been in about the 5th grade before I realized that my mother was not quite the same as other mothers—other sober mothers, that is. Strangely enough, I didn't hate her or anything, I just didn't understand her, or her problem. Later, as a young adult, I even went with her to AA meetings, and to the big Akron AA founder's celebrations, but I still didn't understand it. Sad part is, I don't guess she ever did either. I remember wondering how she could stand missing so much of her life. She must have wondered that too because when I was in high school, she got sober, and stayed that way until her death in 1991. I was living in Florida by then and I remember Dad calling me to come home.

"You're mother's dead," he said simply and without emotion.

"I don't have the money to come home on," I told him truthfully.

"I'll send it," he said. And he did.

To my credit, I bought a plane ticket and came home to the funeral of a woman whose life had been totally interwoven with mine since that September afternoon in Georgia when she and Dad thanked the good doctor for the fine healthy baby she held in her arms.

I stood silently by the grave as they lowered the coffin and tried to feel something—anything—but I could not.

Mom's dead. That's that.

I wish I could lie and say I was devastated, or at least sad about the loss, but unfortunately I cannot. I couldn't wait to get back on the plane and away from Ohio, far away from the freshly dug grave, away from Dad and certainly all the tearful and properly grief-stricken relatives.

"Gary ain't never gonna amount to nothing..."

"Less than nothing..."

"...Had to send him the money to fly home..."

"Don't that beat all..."

"Irene knew it all along... probably why she... uh... used to drink some..."

My father and I had mostly what I considered a good relationship as I was growing up. Of course it wasn't as though I could compare it with any other father—my first one meeting such an untimely death and all. We did all the father-son things and we talked a lot. We never said a whole lot, but we talked just the same. As a family we did a lot of the expected "family things." The trips to Burr Oak Lodge; boating, fishing, horseback riding, nature hikes, the whole nine-yards of "family fun." During those times I do remember being especially happy that my mother did not drink. There was not even a trace alcohol on her breath, and she seemed to be carefree and even looked younger and prettier as she would hike with my father and me through the lush trails of the southern Ohio woods. It was during those times when I would wonder why, if she could lay down that bottle then, that she couldn't simply toss it away forever.

Thankfully, she did.

My dad, as close as we were, had his own set of strict rules for life, especially mine, and even quite a few other people's as well. There was no bending those rules at all. Maybe that's why in time, I figured I might as well just break them all and be done with it. I could never adjust to his concept of the way life should be—which was his way or the highway.

"You're taking piano lessons."

"Don't want no piano lessons."

"Your mother wants you to..."

"I don't want to play the piano."

"Do it anyway. You'll thank us one day."

I never did, of course—thank them, although I did take lessons for awhile. You can imagine how much I learned and how well I play today.

Underlying it all, there began to emerge, probably when I was around the 4th or 5th grade, and certainly continuing into my high school years and beyond, some biting and caustic little remarks which soon became more pronounced and severe until I could no longer ignore them. While neither of my parents would ever think of laying a hand on me in anger, or doing me bodily harm, or be guilty of child abuse as we think of it today, there was a strange cruelty which seemed to come out of nowhere. And, in spite of past efforts to "tune them out," I found myself becoming more and more disturbed by their put-downs and hurtful remarks which seemed to be designed to intentionally cause pain to a boy who did not understand why his parents sought to damage him.

"Why can't you be more like him?" they would ask, when someone in the family or a neighbor would tell of their son making the honor roll, or scoring the winning touchdown at the Homecoming game.

"Look what your cousin Greg did... why don't you do that?"

"Why do you do the stupid things you do?" was a favorite question to which I had no pat answer. Shoot, I had no answer to any question, at least not ones I could offer to my parents at that particular time of my life. The old "Gary won't amount to anything" Chinese torture trick was being dripped into my brain one word at a time.

At the same time, also probably about the 5th grade, I became suddenly aware that school was a royal pain in the butt. I probably even learned that when I flunked first grade, but it somehow became extremely clear to me when I was about ten or eleven.

Is there a pattern beginning to form here?

Is this kid a problem, or what?

To the good sisters at St. Martha's I was nothing short of a holy terror. The ones who still thought there was some redemption in my sorry soul must have spent countless hours and many Hail Mary's trying to get Somebody-Up-There to listen to them about me. I knew there had to be some real bead—moving on my behalf, but I didn't really give a hoot. I let them know that in every possible way I could. And, I came up with some real innovative ways to chip away at the edges of their sanity each and every day. Only thing is, there may have been some of those sisters who were praying that I'd get my "pay-back" in years to come. Well, I'm here to tell you, them prayers were answered big time.

To be truthful, I had to fight very hard against committing the terrible sin of absolutely hating the nuns because, holy or not, some of those wicked old women were just flat-out mean. I'll admit I gave them good reason to be mean most of the time. Oh, all right, all of the time.

The first few years of my life were not much more than a blur. I don't remember any of the exciting Christmas mornings and happy birthday parties other adults would talk about later. I don't recall any bedtime stories, although I'm sure there were some. I had very few "mileposts" and certainly no major events I could look back on, although I swear, even at the risk of shooting my credibility all to heck, I can remember the day President Kennedy

died, even though I was only two months old. I don't know
whether somebody told me how it happened, described the scene,
if I overheard it later, or if I actually have the real memory of that
day, but the image is clearer than any other event in my early life.
I was lying in my buggy in the driveway of our house while my
mother and the next door neighbor wept like babies all over me.

I must have guessed something really bad had happened.

By the time I got into high school, things had gotten progressively worse, in my home, in school, and certainly in my own
muddled head. I was the ultimate band geek—Good grief, played
the tuba yet—at St. Vincent's—St. Mary's High School in Akron,
Ohio. I even wore the customary black plastic rimmed glasses and
girls treated me like I had dirty teeth and bad smelling feet, which
I probably did. The only thing I wasn't was fat. That came later.

I was one of those misfit kids who fit the description usually
written up in the newspaper after a student has gone off the deep
end and robbed the liquor store, offed a teacher or kidnapped
somebody important.

"Fourteen-year old Gary Shawkey, a loner, and as his class-
mates described him, weird and a little strange, walked into the St.
V. auditorium today, put down his Tuba and began to spray paint
the Science teacher with yellow enamel. The spectacled C-student
showed no remorse when several people in the room passed out
from the fumes..."

I got more fun out of imagining things I could do for revenge
and fun than most kids got from the actual acts. The truth was that
I was a loner and a dreamer and I liked being both. I didn't see a
darned thing wrong with either one. I offered no apologies for
projecting my fertile mind into other places and times and I didn't
crave the companionship of my peers.

I liked watching television by myself, and I enjoyed the movies, especially those showing gangsters like Scarface and the other tough guys. I studied Miami Vice carefully, most of the time figuring more money was being made by the drug dealers than by the two main cop characters on the show. Although they did dress rather well for cops and life was certainly good for them, what with the great looking women and all, I couldn't help but wonder if they might be on the take.

World events didn't interest me a whole lot. We had a new president; some peanut farmer from Georgia named Carter. He smiled a lot, and both he and his wife talked funny. Elvis died fat, and I would just lay back and watched the cool Fonzie work his magic on television. The movies were leaning away from my favorite gangster films and showing dancing shit like "Saturday Night Fever" and some goofy thing about outer space called "Star Wars." I didn't pay too much attention to music, even when the Eagles sang "Hotel California." I'd never been to California so there was no way for me to identify with that too much.

Early on, I felt that I was seeking out my own education from watching movies and television and people. And, I knew that money was important in achieving whatever ends I expected to achieve. School was never "where it was at" for me. I didn't care if I never made president of the class or if the teacher complimented or cussed me. It was always the latter anyway. I did belong to the ski club, and was a good photographer, but social graces and being big-man-on-campus were not things I aspired to, although I had to admit the girls liked those guys, which had to be a plus. I had a couple of true friends, and several counterfeit ones. The phonies came because I bought and paid for them. I always had money, primarily because it was easy to find it at home. If I took it out of my mother's purse when she was still drinking, she never missed it because she thought she spent it herself on cheap wine.

If I "borrowed" it from my father's wallet, he thought my mother stole it to feed her alcoholic habit. If there was any accusing done, it was one of them to the other.

Most of the time I didn't even have the good conscience to feel guilty; good Catholic boy that I was.

"Forgive me father for I have sinned..."

Oh sure, and what's so bad about that?

I had developed the power of close observation very early. I watched people the way I watched movies and television. I would pick a person I thought was successful, or was doing things I wanted to do, and I would make mental notes of how he or she did it. This is still true—even today. There is still nothing new under the sun. Success follows a real and true pattern, and once you've got the hang of it, it's a piece of cake. Sometimes it's a fruit cake, or an upside down deal, but a cake all the same.

I enjoy watching those who have "made it" themselves, not those who have had money handed down to them from a rich Daddy, or won the lottery, or lucked into some scam that set him up for life. I have great admiration for people like Donald Trump, Don Lapre and Tony Robbins. Nobody handed anything to them on a platter, or even a paper plate. They went out, grabbed the proverbial bull by the horns and wrestled that sucker to the ground. They made things happen, which in turn, made money fall into their laps and into their bank accounts.

I looked to, and greatly admired, those who knew how to turn rags to riches, water into wine, sow's ears into silk purses, and brainpower into bulging bags of money.

For a while, I confess I even studied the up-and-coming drug dealers while I was attending good old St. V's. Those who hung around the school, and even some in school, drove big cars and flashed fat rolls of bills that would choke a horse, were impressive to say the least. They all appeared—at least most of them—as though they "had it made", and what was more, they looked and acted important. People looked up to them, liked them, or certainly feared them, and offered them unlimited attention. I could do what they did. I figured I could probably sell drugs better than some of the big guys who were doing it. I may not have been on the honor roll, but I was nobody's fool, and in spite of the fancy cars and expensive threads, I was well aware that some of these smartass dude's ended up doing hard time-several times. Others ended up extremely dead. I didn't have to think about it much, to know that I did not want to go to jail, ever. Being dead was not an option for me either. Besides, I also like to think that somehow that sorry, weak conscience of mine kicked in and whispered in my ear that being a drug dealer not only has no future, but it was just not a good thing to do—even for a kid who was desperately searching for something to latch on to.

I was not without major goals however. Actually, I had one burning desire, which probably explained my even toying with the idea of selling drugs. It began long before my short string of recollections did, and it was quite clear and very simple.

I wanted to be rich.

More precisely, I wanted to be very rich, a millionaire—a multi-millionaire even.

I think I knew from the beginning that it wasn't the actual money I craved, although that's the definition most people give when asked what being rich is, and I had no aversion to the green stuff. Heck, I knew that was where it was at.

Somewhere along the way, I even realized that I better make the best of what an education might offer me. By the time I was a senior, my grades had improved and I was even taking a few college courses, some at Kent State and some at Akron University, but unfortunately I did not have the patience to wait all through my college years before getting on with my life. Too many things were waiting over on the other side of the mountain for me to stay put and focused in one place for another four years.

At eighteen I was definitely ready to go forth and conquer the world.

I had always known what I wanted. By the time of graduation I was even admitting it to myself. What I wanted more than anything at that point, and later as well, was what went with being rich. The respect most of the rich can demand—and get. The feeling of success. Independence. Self-worth. And, yes, I'll admit, the money, or at least, what the money could provide which was all of the things I mentioned.

"You'll never amount to nothing, Gary... nothing..."

"Why don't you..."

Now, I don't want to paint the whole family with a discouraging brush. And at the risk of sounding like the boring part of Genesis where this one begot that one, and another begot this one, there needs to be some semblance of who was who in the family.

I'll talk about Aunt Vicki, my mother's sister, first. She was often my rock when everywhere else I stood was shifting sand. She was loving, caring, and her own person. A bit set in her ways and not too flexible at times, but I admired her and I loved her. More importantly, I think, in spite of everything, she loved me.

Everybody should have an Aunt Vicki-if they can survive one like her.

There was Aunt Pam, also my mothers' sister, and Uncle Steve, her husband. They got along real well with Dad and they often came over and played pinochle. Pam's son Greg was another favorite of mine. He was one of those people I would watch very intently. He was my definition of "cool." He always had good jobs, each one more interesting than the last. He was successful and loved adventure, which seemed to follow him around like a stray puppy. I certainly envied him of that.

Aunt Gloria was Aunt Pam's daughter and there was a good feeling in knowing that they both cared about me. They were the ones who always asked how I was—regardless of whatever mess I was in-and they were concerned for my welfare all of the time. I believe they loved me, or at least they did when I would let them.

Gloria proved to be one of the all-time important people in my life, especially when the bad times came. People always say you can tell who your real friends are when you get in trouble-well, bless her heart, Gloria came through for me time and again under circumstances that defy description. She was there for me. I don't know what I would have done without her. Well, yes I do know what I would have done without her. I would have blown my damn brains out, pure and simple. If it had not been for her, and later, my children, I would not be here to write this book or to even breathe air. Talk about leading somebody through the valley of death, well that was Gloria. Now, if that sounds overly-dramatic to you, just wait until I get to those parts where this saint of a woman came riding to my rescue like an angel in the night.

Aunt Vicki, for all her support of me in the past, did not greet me well when I came home for my mother's funeral. In fact, she read the riot act to me.

"You have ruined your Dad's life," she almost hissed at me.

I didn't bother to answer.

"You are such a piece of crap..."

Still, no answer.

"You were the death of your dear mother..."

Another twist of the knife.

Aunt Vicki was never one to NOT have the extreme last word. In her Last Will and very tart Testament, she left a substantial amount of money to various foundations and individuals. At the end of the overly long document, she made it clear that she could still thumb her nose at me from the grave.

"To my nephew Gary, who doesn't care about anything but himself, I leave him one-hundred dollars." She did, however, leave my children something to remember her by, and I am deeply grateful to her for that.

Way to go, Aunt Vicki!

Well, whether it was to "show Aunt Vicki," or to prove my value as a human being to other people as well as myself, or whether it was some strange and innate desire to leap tall buildings in a single bound, I could not wait to get on with life, preferably the one belonging to Gary Shawkey.

First, I needed that almighty money. I went to the well of my father, as I so often had, and would continue to do, well into my adult years.

I'm sure he wanted me to go to college after my graduation from high school, but I would have no part of that. I was too anxious to get on with what I thought was real life. Hardly down the graduation aisle from good old St.Vincent — St.Mary's that I announced to my parents that I wanted to go into business for myself.

I needed a little cash, a few thousand maybe. I thought the Shawkey bank was always open and always ready to provide me with a substantial amount of cash when I needed it. What's more, I didn't need collateral of any kind. My word was good enough. And what kind of a business would a young man just out of high school be capable of doing?

I called myself a photographer, a professional photographer. After all, I took reasonably good pictures. I had a good eye for what composed an interesting concept, and with my father's $5,000 I went out and bought myself a fancy camera, some darkroom equipment, and opened a little studio down on North Main Street in Akron, Ohio.

I hung out my shingle and placed an ad in the newspaper.

"Wanted: Models to work for professional photographer. Be a Star. Good fees with the exciting possibility of contacts with professional agencies."

I gave my phone number and the band geek sat down to wait for the calls-and the beautiful girls-to come rolling in.

And, son-of-a-gun... that's just what they did.

I had hit the flippin' jackpot. I couldn't believe my good fortune. I had never been very successful with women before, but all that changed in the click of a shutter. One luscious voice after another answered my ad and in large numbers and long legs, they showed up at my studio where I snapped photo after photo of them as they looked lovingly into the lens of my brand new camera.

"Look into the camera honey... that's it... fantastic..."

"Just a little more to the left sweet... good girl..."

"Great shot, girl... that'll be your chance at the big time..."

This crap was so easy, I thought. I couldn't believe most of them actually paid me for lavish portfolios I put together for them. I took some pride in the fact that I really wasn't scamming anybody. I was giving them goods for money paid, but heck, it was so easy and so much fun I thought surely there must be either something illegal or sinful about what I was doing.

Oh Lord, if only Sister Martha could see me now. I would show her that the scars on my knuckles had healed where she smacked me with that darn ruler, and what was more important, I was not anywhere near the failure she always predicted I would be.

In fact, I was on the road to total and absolute success. In no time at all I would be making top dollars and those illusive dreams which I had held all through my childhood, were beginning to materialize.

And the women, those beautiful women, just could not seem to get enough of good ol' Gary.

I was convinced that nothing could stop me from achieving my wildest dreams and my most daring fantasies. And, maybe nothing could, but some one did. His name was Bob Fullerton. One fine day, old snappy, dapper Bob, wearing his $400 suits and Rolex watch, simply appeared almost out of thin air. I've tried several times to recall exactly where I met him and under what circumstances, but somehow I keep drawing a blank space. It was probably a bar, or he could have come into my studio. He may have simply fallen right out of a black cloud; I just don't remember. It was only later that I recall paraphrasing a segment in the good book about being kind to strangers, "lest ye may entertain angels unaware," I think was the way it went.

Only problem was, old Bob was sure no angel, so I have to figure I was entertaining the other side of that coin, and smart as I thought I was, I was certainly "unaware" of the likes of the amazing Mr. Fullerton. My first hard and very memorable lesson in my not-yet-wise-enough-life was just beginning. And you know what they say about fools rushing in.

It was like I just couldn't wait to get smacked in the face with that cold, wet sock of experience.

The Second Chapter

BIG BAD BOB
And Other Life-Lesson Teachers

"Every man is a volume,
if you know how to read him."
—Channing

There are those who say that when a person is ready to learn something-anything—there will always be a teacher who shows up to teach it. It may be something spiritual. It may be something philosophical or it may be something that will teach you beyond a shadow of a doubt to steer clear of certain people and certain situations. Still, we never know what we will learn from those who walk—sometimes trample—through our lives.

Well, Big Bob Fullerton appeared bigger 'n life and twice as amazing, ready to teach me some of life's most valuable lessons, both good and bad.

My little photo studio in Akron was doing well, certainly much better than I ever thought it would, and I was satisfied with my growing reputation of doing a good job and offering people excellent value for their money. Of course, my dreams were well beyond that little shop on Main street, but heck, it was a start, and a very good one, if I do say so myself.

One of the first things I remember about Bob was him looking around my studio and asking me how I was doing. I told him I was doing well, and then he asked me if I'd like to do better. Of course I would. Who wouldn't? Before I knew it, I had a business partner. He was that slick and that good.

Bob had a small plane pilot's license and he suggested we do aerial photography. He said we could fly over homes and businesses, take the pictures, then present a package deal to the people to see if they wanted to buy it. Well, of course they wanted to buy it, as he knew they would. I watched that man make his presentations to these people and was absolutely amazed at how they would not only buy, but were almost begging him to allow them to give him their money. I began to think that even if he had given them a bad deal, they would have been so taken by his charm and personality they would have only blamed themselves, and never him. I had never met anybody like Bob before. Since then, I've met a few people from the Big Bob school of Magic Sales, some of whom were way over the line from honesty, but at that point in my life, this was a whole new experience for me.

My dad came in one day while Bob was in the studio and it took him only about two seconds to get Bob's number. For some reason Bob failed to convince my dad that he could walk on water, even though he did it every day with our customers.

"Get away from him," Dad said immediately when we were alone. "That man is bad news and when he ends up behind bars, I don't want you in the next cell."

"He's just an enthusiastic salesman, Dad," I told him, but my protests fell on deaf ears. "He's a hustler and a shyster," Dad insisted. "He's nothing but trouble. Get rid of him."

Well, I wasn't about to do that. My business was flourishing, and thanks to Bob Fullerton, there seemed to be no end to the things I was able to accomplish. It was a heady and addictive feeling to be able to wave your hand over rags and watch them materialize into riches.

It wasn't that I was so naive that I did not see through some of the things Bob did, and the way he manipulated people was both fascinating and a little disturbing. Granted, we were offering them an honest product, perhaps a little overpriced, but as long as the market was willing to bear the cost, I had no problem with it. I was almost mesmerized as I watched him hold customer after customer in the palm of his hand and work his magic on their minds like nobody I had ever seen. Furthermore, I doubt we had one single customer who was not totally satisfied with the product we sold them, and they were willing to recommend us to their friends and relatives. I made mental notes of everything Bob did, dissected his techniques and methods thoroughly because I knew that was the kind of ability a person would have to have in order to build an empire. And, let's face it, since I had been a kid, I knew that's what I wanted—what I had—to do. I could never imagine myself working eight to five in a store or midnight shift in a factory for wages that would barely cover my expenses. I had high hopes, big dreams and the images in my mind did not include being poor or even "comfortable" as some people like to call it.

At this pivotal point in my life, I saw in Bob a man who could teach me far more than I could ever learn in boring Business 101. He was not only an excellent teacher, but he was a heck of an entertainer and there was never a dull moment, regardless of the situation. Learning had never been so much fun or so profitable. I think it was Abraham Lincoln who said, "I will study and get ready and my time will come." Well man, I was getting ready. If it was good enough for ol' Abe, it was good enough for me. Of course, I had to take into consideration that although poor Abe studied and got ready, then met his Maker at the mean end of a revolver, hey, he became the President first.

As I was taking notes on some of Bob's techniques, I realized he sometimes played fast and loose with the truth—more than the regular salesman. He did it in such a way however, that even some of the brightest and most street-smart people could not see it. He seemed to blind them with his fancy footwork and his well chosen words of encouragement. I began to realize though, that if he had based those same techniques on a solid foundation, he could achieve anything he desired. The only thing was, I also came to notice, that Bob desired only the moment, big money, big times and big excitement. Tomorrow or the future, were words not even in his vocabulary, much less part of his overall plan-if he had one. I often tried to talk to him about "building" and he just laughed. The Here-and-Now was his domain, and he took little thought of what would happen after that. If he left a few broken hearts or empty wallets in his wake, he did not seem to give it much thought, and certainly he wasted none of his precious time on regrets and self-recrimination.

It was never all work and no play for Bob either, although with him his work was often his play. We regularly made the rounds of the night spots in Akron and other cities as well. He was a sharp dresser and a big spender. It did not matter that Bob was not movie-star handsome, the women, even the beautiful and classy ones, just flocked to him like magnets. For a young man who had not been a big honcho on campus either in high school or college, this was heady stuff for me, because through osmosis I guess, I was suddenly Mister Popularity as well, and it was sweeter than I had ever imagined.

Having seen firsthand how super selling can be done; I continued to study hard under my slick professor for some time. I took the best of what he was able to show me and put it together with what I felt was a fair shake for the customer and applied it. Just like salve on a wound, the outcome was fantastic. There was no "secret" to it, only specific methods of selling and exceptional techniques that are applied by every super salesman, motivational speaker and every successful entrepreneur. In the second part of the book, I will go into these methods with much more detail.

During this period of time I had also become involved with selling a weight-loss product, a food supplement made by Herbalife International, Inc. As everyone is aware, the weight loss business is a multi-billion dollar business in America. We all look for that magic bullet that will transform us from hefty into slim, trim and beautiful, where life will be perfect and we will sail away on the sea of riches and tranquility. I knew the product worked, and I emphasized its positive points to the people who wanted some help with their weight. I also began to implement some of the sales techniques I learned from Bob. As if by some unbeliev-able magic, I found myself to be a red hot salesman. The product was not, of course, that elusive magic bullet some people hoped it was, but it was effective if used according to the guidelines. Sometimes people with a great deal of weight to lose needed that quick jolt to set them on the right course and people with a few pounds to use found this to be just the right incentive to get them off. Herbalife was not a cure-all, but it helped people at least put themselves on a kind of regimen, which is the first step in weight loss or any kind of self-improvement. I tried to emphasize that to all my customers, along with encouragement and hopefully, some of the "ol' Bob" enthusiasm and conviction.

It worked. By George, it worked like a charm and in no time I had large checks coming in. The way the Herbalife operation worked was somewhat like the Amway system operates. Each salesperson gets ten or twenty; sometimes hundreds or more other people to work under them. Not only do they make a profit off what they sell, but a percentage of the profits from what the others sell. When those twenty or one hundred salespeople recruit ten or twenty more each, you can see how the profits would build up. It not only adds up for the guy who manages to recruit salespeople, but in my case, I took the time to train them in the "Big Bad Bob" theory of selling and it worked like a charm for them as well.

We were all walking in some pretty tall cotton for quite some time and actually I still earn a pretty good little paycheck from the firm foundation I put down way back then.

In addition to the Big Bob factor in my life, there came along another life-changing event. It was one that would bring me all kinds of emotion, including some happiness, but even more pain and misery, but along with one of the greatest joys of my life—a son, Joey.

It was in the late summer of 1984 that I met Debbie. I was out at a campground in a small town just outside of Akron, and I was, at the time, feeling very self-confident and a little cocky, I guess. Life was being good to me for a change and the high hopes I had nurtured all my life were beginning to take some shape. There was a light at the end of the tunnel of my life and it wasn't no danged train. It was a shining opportunity.

That warm summer afternoon, I spotted a rather melancholy looking young woman alone on the edge of the crowd. She looked like she needed a friend. As I approached her, there was such a forlorn countenance about her that I wondered if she ever smiled. To my delight I found out that she did. I was feeling a little smug that I was the one able to bring out that smile. My very first impression was that she was a sweet person, but lonely.

Debbie was, as I had been so many times in my life, kinda on the outside looking in, so I could easily identify with her. Those days were not all that far behind me and I knew the pain and loneliness of being "left out" and feeling isolated. She was some-what overweight and of course, since I was in the business of sell-ing a weight loss product, I was very observant and sensitive to her right off the bat. It was easy to see right from the start that this was not one of the better times in her life. I suppose that was one of the reasons I was drawn to her and why I decided to offer my friendship. She seemed pleased that I had, and in no time at all we were spending a lot of time together. She even made the rounds of the night spots with Bob and me on a couple of occasions, but that was a trio that did not mesh at all. Like my father, Debbie seemed to take an immediate dislike to Bob. Well, let's tell it like it was. She absolutely could not stand the guy. She was one woman-one of the few—who was not charmed in the slightest by the silver-tongued devil. She only saw the last part, and needless to say, encouraged me to drop him like a hot potato. Actually, as time passed, she more than encouraged, she almost demanded that I sever those ties immediately. That should have been a red flag to me. I was never one to take direct orders; especially those deliv-ered much like an ultimatum. Debbie continued to be very demanding and there was no discussing Bob with her at all. In fact, she became quite a bitch about almost everything I did, never missing an opportunity to belittle me or my work and certainly my choice of a best bud. She would not give an inch, and she gave neither me nor Bob the benefit of a doubt. By this time Debbie and I had already moved in together and she became more determined than ever to rid us both of any influence of Bob Fullerton.

It was also about this time that she began to complain even more about my line of work. She did not like me working the Herbalife products. She made it clear, time and again, that she did not consider what I did, "real work."

"That whole thing's a scam," she said, using herself as a failed example. "It didn't work for me. You are misleading people with it. It's dishonest and I hate that. Surely, you can do better than that. I know you can do something else, so why are you still doing this?"

I assured her that there was nothing dishonest or even misleading about selling the product. I tried again and again to point out that a lot of people had been helped by it. All were not successful, but they were promised-and given-their money back if it did not work for them. As far as I was concerned it worked for those who worked with it. So far, scientists have not come up with a pill that does all the work for you, one that melts off the fat without any effort whatsoever on your part. I tried to tell her this over and over, but Debbie was not one to listen when she had already made up her mind. And, not only had she made up her mind about Herbalife and the illustrious Mister Fullerton, she seemed not to be all that keen on me anymore either.

Both the diet pills and Fullerton had to go, she kept insisting. It was as simple, and as complicated, as that.

Looking back, I'm sure I would have snipped the frayed threads that bonded me to Bob long before I did, had Debbie and my dad stopped yapping and nagging about him so much. I had planned to cut the ties in my own time and in my own way. Debbie did not have a corner on "stubbornness." I could hold my own in that department any time. The time had come however, for me to sever the relationship with Bob and I set about to doing just that. It was not because Debbie insisted I do it, but because I had already picked his brain for everything I needed, and everything he had to give anyway. I knew I could incorporate that remarkable "selling" part I had learned from him into a good, solid base and build on it. I wanted something would stand, and not something that would fall to pieces at the first little jolt. Bob's whole concept of building a business was like a house of cards. One wrong move and the whole thing would come tumbling down, something that did not seem to worry or even concern him in the slightest. He would, I knew, move on to the next station in his life without a single glance back over his shoulder. Unlike Bob however, the future was something that I had given a lot of thought to, and my plans did not include being here today and gone tomorrow. I didn't want to have to leave town in a mad rush because the hounds were snipping at my heels. When I left a place, I wanted it to be because I was moving on to something bigger and better with every step I took. And I wanted the steps to be upward and onward, not running for my bloody life.

"Why don't you get a real job?" Debbie asked one night for the hundredth time.

"A real man would get a real job."

So, I did.

The Third Chapter

The Journey Continues

"When you find that flowers and shrubs
will not endure a certain atmosphere,
it is a very significant hint to the human creature
to remove it from that neighborhood."
—Mayhew

To tell you the truth, I blame myself for "giving in" to the pressures that Debbie put on me. Not where it concerned Bob Fullerton, but in the Herbalife business. I was reaching the place where it was really beginning to pay off and when Debbie complained about it, I reminded her that she didn't have any trouble taking the money that came in.

"Money could come in from something else, too," she said. "You can do other things."

Other things. What other things? She had no answer for that. Again I tried to tell her that I believed in the Herbalife product completely, and second, I was good at selling something I believed in. I thought Herbalife and I was a perfect combination, and I still believe if I'd followed my instincts then, I could have saved everybody a lot of grief. I honestly felt that I had finally stumbled upon my life's work and I was truly convinced that in no time at all, I would be able to achieve that all-important dream I'd been harboring for so long. I would be rich. I would be successful, and quite likely I would be gone... from Debbie.

Debbie talked about the future and I didn't even want to consider the future with her, but it seemed that plans were already underway. Debbie was relentless in her pursuit of what she deemed to be my happiness and her future, which she believed were one and the same. I don't recall exactly how it happened, but I suppose it was during one of my weaker periods that I finally gave in to her nagging, went out, and got a "real job".

I went to work as a cook at Bob Evans. You can't get much more real than that.

Before too long however, I was moving up the Bob Evans corporate ladder, riding that sausage gravy train right to the top-in a manner of speaking. When they gave me a position as a trainer, Debbie was beside herself with pride. I was just beside myself, period. It was, I kept thinking, a way to make a living, and having undertaken the job, I figured I should do it as well as possible.

And, I did.

The management was so impressed with my abilities that in a few months I was offered a job in Georgia as a trainer, with more money, travel expenses, and another slice of what Debbie felt was prestige and possibly "the good life."

"We'll have a great time down there..." Debbie said, obviously pleased that we were moving up in the world. I was a little disturbed with the pronoun "we" she used all the time, but things seemed to be progressing in a certain direction whether I wanted them to or not.

The pressure continued for us to "get married" especially since I would be moving out of state. I couldn't figure out how it seemed to be all right if we lived together in Ohio, but if we moved away, we needed to be married.

My objections were in the minority however, and before I knew it, the two of us were standing shoulder to shoulder at the courthouse in downtown Elyria repeating some very somber-sounding words in front of a bored-looking judge which made it all legal and binding-at least for the time being.

As soon as we could get our stuff together we took off south. Sometimes I almost came close to trying to make it work out—I think. Then I would come to what I thought were my senses, the old restless spirit would kick in and I would find myself wishing with all my heart for the day when I would be able to find the courage to walk out the door alone.

I don't want it to appear that I didn't love Debbie at all. I did, and at that time and at that place, she was important to me. When she became pregnant, I tried very hard to be happy about it, but the truth of the matter was, I panicked. I saw it only as a tighter twist around my already suffocating neck. The thought of a life-time with Debbie became more and more of a thing I knew I did not want-could not tolerate. I was barely into my 20's and I want-ed more out of life than what I had, or what "we" had, but I didn't know what, where, or who the heck 'more' was.

Even before Joey was born I knew I wanted out. Afterwards, I couldn't seem to get into the swing of being the good father and the good husband—especially the latter.

Having learned from the best-my old friend, Bob—I had no problem at all cheating on the little woman. I don't think I even rationalized that it was partly her fault and that it was just something I needed from time to time, I just plain old cheated because I wanted to. No more, no less. Not complicated at all.

The truth was, I remembered ol' Bob standing at some bar and looking over the crop of young things, and he'd say, "Hey, there's one I want," and he'd go get her, or stranger yet, she'd come to him. Seemed like a good plan to me, and later I put snappy dapper Bob's examples into motion every chance I got.

Debbie knew all was not well. She knew she was being cheated on, but she rode out each little storm by causing an even bigger one of her own. In time she would figure that was what "was sauce for the goose, was sauce for the gander"—which in plain English meant that she'd just cheat on the old cheater. I don't know if she figured it would "show me," or make me jealous or what. Actually, it made no difference to me one way or another, which seemed to infuriate her more than ever.

Being a so-called "big shot" trainer for Bob Evans did not bring in enough money for an expanding family, so I hired Debbie as cashier/hostess. Now we had the pleasure of fighting all day (or night, depending on the shift) at home, and fighting the other shift at the restaurant. We could have written a book on how not to have a successful marriage, except those people who might be looking for that kind of advice already seemed to have an innate ability to mess up their lives without instructions from anybody else.

Faced with Debbie's pregnancy and the continuing turmoil in our marriage, I did what any brilliant and successful father-to-be would do.

I quit my job.

I just simply walked out without looking back. Why did I do that? Darned if I know. I didn't know then and I don't know now. I just did. But I wasn't without work for long. In a very short time I had a brand new job—as a roofer.

Even thinking about that whole deal still makes me sweat. It's not real hard to imagine how crappy it would be to climb up a ladder onto a blistering hot roof with that Georgia sun that probably registered at least 120 degrees, beating down on your back, and pour on hot tar, which was well over boiling temperature, and spread it around. But hey, I stuck—pardon the pun—with it. I stayed four-and-a-half hours, working full tilt and sweating like a fattenin' hog.

"You did what?" Debbie was horrified.

"I'll get another job..."

"And quit it too?" she snapped.

"I might..."

They say things always get worse before they get better, but in our case, things got worse before they got worse than that. The fact that I got a job at Shoney's right away did little to comfort the pregnant lady. She no longer believed there was any security in old Gary and the nagging that had been unbearable before, got steadily worse.

The only plus in a huge pile of negatives was the birth of our son. Joe came into the world a wonderful little boy, a good baby, healthy and handsome, with the potential to be president if he wanted to. At least that's what people always say when a little boy comes into the world. "Just think, he could grow up to be president." I can't recall though, anybody ever saying that of me, although they very well could have, given the strange aspects of my early days.

Once again, I hired Debbie to work for me at the restaurant. We worked opposite shifts so we could take turns caring for Joey, which worked out well for two reasons. One, I didn't have to see Debbie hardly at all, and two, I was extremely privileged to get to know this special little creature who had come somewhat uninvited into my life. Because I got the chance to be a 100 per cent caretaker when I was with him, the time we had together became very important, and I would like to think that we did the "bonding" thing that the so-called experts tell us is so necessary. Maybe it is, and if it is, I believe we were able to do that very thing.

One thing for sure, Joey didn't have to work hard to capture his old man's heart. In spite of all else that seemed wrong with my life; Joey, with his wide toothless smile, was certainly one of the shining bright spots in my not-so-happy world. I knew then, and I think Joey even knew, that whatever happened to the family as a unit, the position he had taken in my life would not change. In the months and years to come, I would let him down, of course, from time to time and I could never find an excuse good enough for that. I would not and sometimes could not, always do right by him, but during those first months, Joey and I became a fantastic team.

What Joey didn't know though, and what I certainly did not discuss with him, was that I was looking for a way to get out of the marriage to his mother once and for all, because by the time he was six months old, I had not only made this momentous decision, I had met somebody else as well. I had also met all the extra baggage, which included a serious illness, and a good-for-nothing husband, that she was carrying in her life.

Of course, that was just what I needed to really complicate my already mucked-up existence.

The Fourth Chapter

Sweet Georgia Peach

*"Grace was in her steps,
heav'n in her eye,
In every gesture dignity and love"*
—Milton

I t was one of those nothin' little dresses.

You know the kind. It's the ones some of those southern women can just throw on and look for all the world like sweet vanilla ice cream and all the sugar and spice girl things that cause some men to go bonkers over a woman.

Worked for me.

The first time I saw her walking into Shoney's Restaurant in Griffin, Georgia that warm Spring morning, I was an absolute goner. I could not believe my good fortune when I discovered she was one of the waitresses where I had come to work as the manager.

She could have asked for the moon, or my head on a platter, and she woulda got it.

The soft, thin, flowery dress was long and flowing, full at the bottom but just snug enough through the middle and cut just low enough to show off her drop-dead gorgeous figure. She had unbelievably beautiful skin and one of those soft lilting accents that gave her a certain grace that usually comes from some long dead ancestor who lived back in the Old South.

She had her long, straight, light brown hair pulled back off her face and even though she approached the front of the restaurant with her chin held high, I wasn't so blinded by her overall appearance that I didn't notice somewhere in the depth of her dark blue eyes that she was trying to hide something.

I guessed it was some kind of pain.

I guessed right, but it was not the kind of pain caused by the diabetes which I later discovered that she had contracted when she was ten. It was one of those man-made pains, inflicted upon her "only when she needed it" by one of the good old boys who had been brought up to "keep a woman in her place" by whatever means necessary.

"I want to be real honest with you," she said, her soft voice tinged with some nervousness during one of the first conversations we had. "I've had this old diabetes all my life and there may be times when I might have to miss some work, but I'll do the best I can."

I didn't give a darn.

"Don't worry about it," I said simply, hoping she didn't pick up on the fact that I was a goner. Odds were though, I thought, she did. In addition to being all that pretty, I could tell that she was very smart, too.

"Here's my life, my heart and my soul. Take them too, if you want 'em."

That's what I thought that morning, but I didn't say it. That's what she did, however, without even realizing it, and I couldn't have been more pleased.

If I could lie and say that I was disturbed that I was a married man, already making plans to make even more plans with a woman equally married, then I would—but that was not the case. It just seemed like the most natural thing in the world. The word "cheating" did not even enter into it. That was what I did with someone I cared about for the moment. This woman literally zapped me right in the heart. I always thought love at first sight was some goofy kid thing, and there I was, acting just like a goofy kid.

I knew the first time I saw Teresa—that we had a future together of some kind. The only thing I didn't know was how turbulent, how wonderful, and how short it would be. It wouldn't have mattered anyway. I wouldn't have backed off if someone had drawn graphic pictures of the pain for me. It was indeed something I believed at the time that was "meant to be." The dreamer in me never stopped dreaming, even when the dreams became nightmares.

I wish I could recall that I felt sorry for Debbie, or about what I was doing to her, but that wasn't the case either. We had gotten married simply because it was "the thing to do," and because her parents, whom I loved dearly, expected I would "do the right thing," even though their "right thing" and my "right thing" were not exactly parallel to one another.

I don't know what would have happened if Teresa had not come along when she did. I doubt that I would have stayed in the marriage much longer. I have to wonder too, what would have happened to Teresa if I hadn't come into her life when I did. Would she have been better—or worse off—I honestly don't know. I only know that for a time, we had it all, and more.

Teresa's husband Jerry had suffered a bad fall some years before and was on disability. Actually, his claimed disability was simply an excuse not to work. At least, that was the way I saw it. He was one lazy dude, what I believe some call a "real go-getter." His only job consisted of being available when the wife gets off from work--then he "goes and gets her," which is what makes him a "go getter." His disability also didn't stop him from beating the crap out of her every chance he got.

"He was drunk, Gary..."

"I don't give a rat's butt if he was... he's got no reason to beat you... and if it happens again..."

The first time she came to work with bruises on the side of her face I was ready to kill somebody.

"What happened to you?" I asked, as though it was my business. After all, I had a wife and son to think about. I needed to be worrying about their welfare, not this remarkable creature that was beginning to take over most of my thoughts, my plans and dreams of a future.

Having no right of course, did not stop me.

"Oh... that..." she said, touching her cheekbone. "It's nothing... I'm just a clumsy doofus sometimes..." Her face reddened as she turned away from me.

"Hey... hey..." I said. "Don't lie to me... You can't con a con, you know."

She managed a faint smile as she took a couple of steps down the back hall by the kitchen. I reached out and took her arm and turned her around to face me. I reached up and touched the dark bruise on her face, and she winced.

"Did that son-of-a-gun hit you?"

He was the typical red-neck who was just stupid enough to be dangerous.

At first she was going to deny it again, but her eyes told it all before she managed to turn them away from me. I couldn't help myself. I pulled her into my arms and held her close for a long time without saying anything. I could feel her heart beating like a scared rabbit against my chest.

Finally, I held her at arms length and made her look at me.

"This is not going to happen any more... He is not going to beat you again. I won't let it happen," I promised her. It was a promise of course—I wasn't able to keep because I wasn't in charge of Butthole.

"He didn't mean..." she began, the next time she came in bruised and battered. Suddenly, I was angry at her. How dare she start to defend a man who would hit her, then try to make her feel like it was "all right."

"I don't ever want to hear you coming to his defense again," I said, my voice more harsh than I meant for it to be. "From now on, when there is a problem of any kind... you just come to me and I'll fix it... I promise... now will you do that?"

She swallowed hard and I thought she was going to start crying.

"If he just didn't drink..." she tried once more to defend him.

"But he does drink..." I shot back. "And he gets off on beatin' up on women..."

"I know... but sometimes I just make him so mad..."

"You could never make anybody that mad," I said, shaking my head. "I would never lay a hand on you in anger and I won't let anybody else do that either..."

"Gary... you can't be talking like that... we're both married," she said. "You've got a little boy..."

"I know... but you know I'm not happy, and I sure as heck know you're not..."

She shook her head, trying to dismiss both me and the conversation.

"Admit it," I said, but she looked down at her feet, still trying to avoid eye contact with me.

"Gary, please..." she began, and stopped in mid sentence.

"Come on now..." I said as I leaned over and kissed her on the forehead. "We both know what we want. We want each other. It's as simple as that. Let ol' Gary take care of you..."

And, she did.

I promised her life would be better. And sometimes, it was. I promised I would take care of her forever, that I would never let anything bad ever happen to her again.

I lied.

The Butthole did beat Teresa a couple more times and each time I exploded into a rage. Debbie and I had reached an impasse in our lives and I knew—and I think she knew, too—it was just a matter of time, days maybe, before we'd have to hang it all up for good.

At the same time, I knew there was no way on God's green earth I was going to stand for Teresa being a punching bag for that stupid heathen.

"That's it..." I told her when she came in one morning with a black eye behind her oversized sunglasses.

"Gary..." she began, but I put my fingers to her lips and told her not to say another word. By now, I was even more of a goner than I had been that first day I saw her. She had become almost an obsession with me. I wanted to take care of her, protect her, make her life wonderful, and most of all, to love her.

And, wonder of all wonders, I believed she wanted the same things.

"How long would it take you to get packed?" I asked then, grabbing her by the shoulders. Her eyes widened and she frowned. She thought I was crazy, and she may have been right.

"I... I don't know..."

"Fifteen minutes... twenty... half-hour... how long?"

"Gary..." she couldn't seem to believe I was serious.

"Come on..." I took her by the elbow and guided her toward the back door of the restaurant.

"Gary...we can't... you're the manager here... and I'm married..."

"So am I."

"I know that..."

As we reached the back door, I took her in my arms and kissed her. I then put my index finger under her chin and told her just to hang in there for a little longer.

"What are you going to do, Gary?" she asked; her eyes wide.

"I'm going to do what has to be done..."

"Gary..."

"Teresa...there's nothing more to be said," I told her. "Everything's been said that needs to be. Now we need some action, and I aim to take action..."

"You're not going to do something foolish, are you?" she asked, her voice full of concern.

"Foolish...?" I repeated. "Hey, I don't know foolish from smart. Guess it depends on who's doing the lookin'. You just sit tight and I'll see you in a couple of days..."

"But where are you going?" she asked. "Are you quitting your job...?"

"I'll tell you when I get back, and yes I am," I answered both her questions.

I kissed her again and took off like the proverbial bat. Actually, that kinda describes the kind of freedom I was feeling, even before I was actually free.

That night, I went home driving a U Haul rental truck. I told Debbie to load up what she wanted to take back to Ohio. By the time she got over the shock of my insane suggestion, she began to gather her things, Joey's few possessions, as well as most of mine, and threw them unceremoniously into the truck. She punctuated each load with new and more obscene descriptions of what I could do with myself and exactly what kind of crap I was made of.

She wasn't far off the mark, but I didn't give a darn.

I followed Debbie and Joey in the U Haul truck as they drove Debbie's car 1,100 or more miles back north. We drove straight through with as few stops and as few words as possible. Joey, mercifully, slept most of the way.

It was early morning when we pulled into the driveway at her parent's home in Elyria. I helped unload the truck and climbed back into the cab without a second look. I'm not even sure I said goodbye to Joey, although at that point in his life, I doubted he lost much sleep over it. I took only a few minutes to see my parents, and ask for more money, and then I was gone again.

I headed back south as fast as the rental truck would go and it moved pretty well. I guess if they put governors on them, they missed this one because several times I watched the needle move into the 80 and 90 MPH section. I drove the entire round trip without taking a shower, shaving, or even taking much time for bathroom duties. I was a man in a hurry because I knew exactly what I wanted and how I was going to get it. Upon arriving at my destination I turned in the truck and with a little money I'd squirreled away, and some I'd borrowed off first one and another, I bought a $300 Chevy junker with an $800 stereo system.

I went back to Shoney's and once again asked Teresa how long it would take her to pack her things.

"Where have you been?" she asked, ignoring my question.

"Ohio..."

She wasn't sure I was saying what I was saying.

"I moved Debbie and the baby back home..." I said.—"For good."

In spite of her effort to conceal it, I saw a distinct look of relief, mixed with some pleasure cross her face.

"How long to pack?" I asked again.

"Not long..." she answered.

As we drove up to the old green and white trailer where she lived with Jerry, I could see the apprehension growing in her as it turned into fear, bordering even on some terror.

"Gary... I'm not sure... what he'll do..."

"Well, if I can't handle him I don't deserve you..."

As I stopped the car, Jerry stepped out of the trailer and stood by the steps as he watched me get out of the car. Then as Teresa opened the door on her side, he ordered her in the house.

"She'll be getting her things," I said, as I watched his eyes narrow into long, angry slits.

"The heck she will," he answered.

I indicated with my head for Teresa to go toward the trailer door as I approached Jerry. He started to reach out toward her but I caught his arm and she dashed inside the trailer. When he started to go in, I indicated very strongly to him that it might not be the best idea for him to do that.

At first I thought he wasn't going to listen, but whatever common sense he had— seemed to kick in as he stood watching Teresa come out with a small suitcase and a couple of brown grocery bags full of stuff.

"You ain't gonna get away with this, Miss High and Mighty with your big shot boyfriend here..." he said, his voice low and threatening. "I aim to make sure you're plenty sorry for what you're doin'... and you know I can do that..."

"You'll do nothing, Butthole, unless you go through me..." I hissed at him.

"That might be possible, a pleasure even," he answered, stepping back slightly but still glaring in my direction. If looks could have killed, I would have been one dead puppy, as would Teresa.

"No, it's not possible at all..." I assured him then, and strangely enough he seemed to agree, if not verbally, at least he didn't act on any objections he might have had.

We were several miles away from the old trailer at the edge of the woods before Teresa finally spoke.

"I can't believe we're doing this...I mean we are just plum crazy... out of our cotton pickin' minds crazy..."

"Believe it," I said.

"We just... did it... didn't we?"

"Yes, we did."

"But, people don't do things like that... at least people I know don't. I don't..."

"I do..." I answered as I reached over and took her hand. "And, you know what sweet Georgia girl... so do you. You just did!"

For a few minutes she sat as though deep in thought as I headed the old Chevy down the highway, putting more and more distance between our past lives and our future ones. Then she looked over at me and gave me one of those smiles of hers that always destroyed me.

"Do you have any idea what you are getting yourself into...?" she said.

I smiled back at her and nodded. "Yes, I do..." I assured her. "And I think I'm happier than I've ever been in my life..."

"I'm not exactly a prize, you know..." she insisted, making a wry face. "I'm sick a lot with this darned diabetes I've got... you know how much work I missed and how mad you got... firing me even, for goodness sake..."

"I hired you back every time, didn't I?"

She nodded; pointing out to me that the number was exactly three times that I had fired her. I reminded her that I had hired her four times, which showed my true colors.

"I'm not much fun when I'm sick," she added almost apologetically.

"Are you fun when you're not sick?"

"Oh heck yes," she answered throwing her head back against the seat and laughing out loud. "I am more fun than a barrel of monkeys and a whole bunch purtier..."

I laughed too and agreed whole-heartedly about her being lots prettier.

"Where're we going, crazy man?" she asked then, moving over closer to me as she turned on the radio, keeping the volume down so we could talk.

"How does Daytona Beach sound to you?"

"Sounds like a good place to go..."

I put my arm around her then and drew her even closer as I watched the center line move beneath the car that was taking us to our future.

She snuggled up against me and asked me if I thought we had done the right thing.

"No!" I answered. "I've had it up to here with 'the right thing'. I'm done with that crap. From now on I'm only doing the good things, no talk about right thing, wrong thing... just the good things, and I can tell you what, Georgia girl, that this is gonna be one great thing from start to finish."

"Gary..." she said, her words muffled against my shoulder. "Do we love each other?"

"We do," I said, and I meant it with all my heart.

"I'm glad," she came back. "I'm very, very glad." I could tell she meant it too.

After awhile she became pensive again as she studied the side of my face closely as we crossed the Georgia line.

"Gary... what'll we do... if I get sick...?"

"You won't..." I said confidently. "I won't let you. I'll make you take some vitamins, and exercise and I'll make you eat right and the first thing we're going to do when we get to Daytona is find a good doctor who can help you get on the right track..."

"I don't like doctors," she answered quickly, her face becoming sullen. "And I'm not even sure there are any good ones..."

"Why do you say that?"

"Doctors are the reason I've got diabetes in the first place..."

"How do you figure that?"

"My Dad told me," she answered. "He said when I was ten, I got some kind of pancreas problem and I had to be taken to emergency. There were two of us kids in the emergency room at the same time and the other one had high sugar. The doctor got us mixed up and gave me medicine that the other kid was supposed to get, and it caused my pancreas to shut down. That's why I'm a diabetic today and why I have so darn much trouble. I hate it... and it was all their fault..."

"Yeah hon, but you can't judge all doctors by that one... I'm sure you've been helped by doctors..." I tried to reassure her.

"No..." she said quickly. "They're all a bunch of quacks...and besides they all charge a fortune... we don't have no money..."

"I got $3,000 from my Dad... and I've got a little of my own," I told her. "That'll last until I get a job."

"You really want me to see a doctor, don't you?" she said. I could tell she was genuinely touched.

"Of course I do. We'll try to find you one of the very best of the quacks in Florida and see if he can help you to keep this miserable stuff under control," I said. "I don't know a lot about it, but I've heard if you do what you are supposed to, it can be controlled very well..."

"You mean... like the 'right thing'?" She said, her voice tinged with some sarcasm as she leaned over to make me look her in the eyes.

I looked closely at her and shook my head. "Not the same 'right' thing I was talking about before..." I insisted.

"Is too," she came back.

"Not... Not..."

"Well, whatever, I hate giving in to this crap," she said, pushing her small frame back against the back of the seat. "I don't even like to admit I have it, much less mess with that darned needle and the stupid diet... The idiot doctors won't even let me drink or have any fun... I never asked them if drugs were OK since I figure most doctors live on them anyway..."

"Teresa..." I began. "I want you to take care of yourself...You don't need to be drinking or doing no drugs. You're signing your own death warrant when you do."

"Well, you're no fun..." she said with a gentle yet accusatory tone...

"Oh yes I am," I insisted. "But I still want to take care of you..."

"I don't need taking care of, old friend," she said quietly as she slid back close to me again. "I need to be cared about..."

"No problem..." I said, smiling again in her direction. I was suddenly aware how little I'd smiled or laughed in the past several months. Now, I could feel all the tension draining away from what had been my muddied up life, and in its place was a pure stream of what just might possibly pass for happiness.

"Another thing..." she added slowly. "I need to be loved."

"Easy," I answered quickly. "Easiest thing in the world..." I leaned over to kiss her softly on the cheek, then remembered a song I'd heard a month or so before. It was Kris Kristofferson with a great line that said 'loving her was easier than anything I've ever done before', and I knew then and there, that was exactly the way it would be for Teresa and me.

And, it was.

The Fifth Chapter

Happily Ever After??

"There is a difference between happiness and wisdom;
he that thinks himself the happiest man really is so;
but he that thinks himself the wisest,
is generally the greatest fool."
—Colton

Goodbye, Georgia!

To tell the truth, the day me and Teresa left Georgia and our former lives behind, I guess we were both foolish enough to believe that "love would find a way" and all that good stuff, but of course that's seldom the case, even if it seemed that way for a while.

Some of those days which followed were, for want of a better word, golden.

I remember thinking how maybe I could just perform miracles, make Teresa well and we would not have a care in the world. Not too long after we got to Florida, I went out and bought her a little blue Camaro. She was absolutely flabbergasted. She danced around the pretty little car and kept running back to hug and kiss me, and I remember thinking at the time that we must be the two happiest people in the entire universe.

Heck, maybe at that time and that place, we were. Who's to say?

I made money and we spent it. I borrowed money and we spent that. I talked people out of money and we spent that-and more. I tried several ventures, and misadventures that were questionable to say the least, each one more successful than the other. We traveled around Florida, Georgia, Alabama and South Carolina, and wherever else the winds of fortune and fun took us. I had my own company called "Dixieland Productions," where I put on fireworks displays. So what if I didn't know what the crap I was doing. Just so those who hired me didn't know that I didn't know, I could get away with charging big bucks. Even the name had kind of a dubious distinction. Sometimes I still worked at "real jobs," including driving a cab, and finally I even went back to working in another Shoney's restaurant, this one in Birmingham. Again, I impressed my bosses so much they gave me my own restaurant in Cullman, Alabama.

This might be it, I thought. Teresa and I just may become regular old married folks. We even rented a house in a nice section of Cullman, and for a time, a very short time, both of us seemed to have settled down fairly well. Of course my entrepreneur business was still ongoing. I still did fireworks displays. I was even beginning to know what I was doing at times. People almost got their money's worth when they hired me. I did balloon displays, skydiving, banner pulling and the bucks were rolling in like summer thunder.

We still spent 'em as fast as heat lightning.

Our new life there lasted about four-and-a-half months. One day, we just sold everything we had-you know, like the good china and the real silver tea sets and the Chippendale couch-yeah, and we did the only thing sensible people would do. We bought us a darn motorcycle. Ain't that what regular folks do?

Now, before you start figuring me for a complete idiot, think about it. While you were riding down the road in your ten-year old beater that needed tires and new tie-rod ends, on your way to a job you literally hated, which you had to keep to pay for a crappy house that needed a new roof and wasn't anything like you dreamed of having, that you shared with a wife who nagged you, and children who neither respected nor give a crap about you, remember ol' Gary here. He has just walked out of his job as a Shoney's manager. He's a bit overweight and certainly overdrawn, but hey, he's got this great looking woman behind him on this brand new Harley, and she is holding on to him for dear life and because she loves him and because she wants to be with him more than anyone else. They are zipping down that black ribbon of highway on their way to sunny Florida without a darn care in the world.

Admit it, you saw us that day. You saw us pass you on the road just before you turned off to go to your crappy job. You wished you were me, and heck, I wished you weren't. Now, which one of us was the most pleased with themselves?

Now of course, in retrospect, I'll admit as well, that I have to look at this particular scenario and know for sure that Teresa and I were both only about three points ahead of total insanity. Still, it seemed quite natural at the time. Natural for us, that is. This is also a good time to point out that a person with my background, if you take all this into consideration, would not be a great candidate for success of any kind. The so-called sensible folks would surely shake their well-groomed heads and click their tongues against their teeth as they remarked about how that Shawkey boy was "never gonna amount to anything." Fact is, that Shawkey boy was trouble with a capital "T." Any thought of him ever being any kind of success was flat-out laughable. And believe me, plenty of them were laughing out loud, except of course, for the ones whose money I'd 'borrowed' and squandered. They seldom laughed much at the mention of my name, or even at the thought of me.

The reason I am not reluctant to tell these things is quite simple. I want people to know how "off the wall" and "off the mark" I was before I even began to walk a straighter financial line and achieve any semblance of success. Oh, I suppose the potential was always there, but there was no discipline and no kind of a plan. I think maybe more of Big Bad Bob rubbed off on me than I planned for it to. Furthermore, my goals, which were still not out of sight, were never mapped out. I had just planned to be rich. There was no business design drawn up, no real formula or loosely drawn blueprint. Even when I told myself that I was gonna "do it," I still had no clue as to where I would begin. I was on that right track somewhat though, when I was with Herbalife, but now that was almost a faded memory. Still, I think the fact that I got my first taste of what real success could be during that time, inspired me to try, try, fail, fail, and try again. If I could have zeroed in on some definite direction, I think I could have parlayed a growing business into a great one, a long time ago, but I have to believe that things have a way of working out in their own time, according to whatever fate and a lot of hard work brings you.

I figured that if anyone who was as loosely organized—or not organized at all—and anyone who pulled the foolhardy stunts I did, and rolled with the self-inflicted punches as I had, could rise above all the shit I walked through and still come out smelling like the well-known rose, then anybody ought to be able to ride the success wagon uphill and all the way to the top, even if there was a missing wheel or two.

Then again, who the heck knows?

All I did know was that each time I did some of those very wild things; things still had a way of working out. I certainly did not lead a charmed life, or things would never have gotten so bad for me at times. I doubted I had a guardian angel, although I must have had, else I would have been washed away in the flood of ignorance and confusion I so often waded through. What I came to believe, actually what I always believed, was that things will take a turn for the better, that just up ahead is the end of the rainbow where I will find the pot of $100 bills; that sooner or later my luck would change.

It was not sooner.

Teresa and I went first to Daytona, where we'd gone when we left Georgia that first time. It was a special place for us and when we hit the beach, all the old familiar things fell back into place and neither of us had any regrets about leaving what most people would consider a somewhat stable environment.

We got us a tent and we slept in that most of the time, sometimes in wooded areas near the beach, sometimes in campgrounds, wherever we could put down the stakes. Most of the time, life was good. Any time we got bored with an area, we'd move on to another. That's how we came to be in Orlando when Teresa began feeling extremely sick. After one long night of partying we got a motel so we could sleep in a real bed for a change.

"I feel like crap," Teresa said when she woke up.

"No wonder," I came back at her. "You really put it away last night."

She made a face in my direction, rolled over in the bed and as her feet hit the floor, so did every thing she'd eaten for the past 24 hours. My first thought was to take her to the hospital but she assured me she'd be all right once she was up and around. Only problem was, she didn't get up or around for the rest of the day. It was more than a week before I finally convinced her to go to the nearest emergency room just so they could have a look at her.

I cooled my heels out in the waiting room as she went into one of the examining booths. I thought she'd never come back. I kept asking what was going on but nobody knew, or nobody would tell. I ended up pacing the floor, wondering if it was something really bad. I found myself hoping they would admit her. At least they could find out why she had been so darned sick.

She was pale when she came out and I ran over to her.

"You OK?" I asked. "Did they give you anything..."

"Yeah," she answered, as she studied my face. "I'm all right. They gave me some crackers..."

"Crackers?" My God, what did we have here, a real Mayo Clinic. Big medicine, crackers. "Why the heck would they give you crackers?"

"They settle my stomach..."

"And, that's it..." I was getting really ticked. What kind of a deal was this anyway?

"That's it," she answered, almost nonchalantly, then cocking her head to one side added with an absolutely straight face. "Oh yeah... and I'm a little bit pregnant..."

At first, the words didn't soak in, then without thinking where I was, I picked her up in a bear hug and swung her around in the hall, kissing her half-smirking face and yelling like a crazy man. Finally, she could hold back no longer either. She let her face break into a big smile and she began hugging me and laughing, both of us acting like fools who had not seen each other in years.

"Don't you think that is just about the most wonderful news you've ever heard in all your born days?" she asked then. Her face was radiant and her eyes sparkled with the new found knowledge of the baby that was growing inside her.

"This is going to be the best time of our lives..." she said, almost bursting with the joy she felt. "You'll see..."

"Did they say you were all right... I mean physically... the diabetes and all...?"

She shrugged. "Guess so... we didn't talk much about it. No point in spoiling one of the happiest times of my life talking crap like that..." Her smile had turned into a frown and I thought it best not to follow that line of communication.

"I told you..." she insisted firmly as she grabbed on to my arm and held it tightly. "We will be all right. You. Me. And this baby..." She took her other hand and laid it on her stomach and looked up at me with happiness such as I had ever seen all over her pretty face.

"She will be the most wonderful baby in the world..."

"She?" I questioned.

"She." Teresa insisted. "I know she's a girl. I can tell. I can feel it. I know."

I never argued with her about it, and of course she was right. She did know.

The next seven-and-a-half months were a mixture of heaven and hell, with a lot more of the latter than the former.

There were times when we were so happy we couldn't believe it was us—then we'd be so miserable that we knew it couldn't be anybody but us.

The roller coaster ride was a thrill-a-minute until the wheels started flying off. Then with each passing day we wondered if we'd make it through. We spent more time in and out of hospital emergency rooms than we did our little apartment I'd rented when we found out the baby was coming.

She was usually too exhausted to walk on the beach, and any thought of sex was out of the question. She was either sick, asleep, or off in another world where I couldn't seem to go. Looking back, I think she may have been afraid she wouldn't live long enough to bring the baby into the world. She even did some of the things the quack doctors told her and she tried to follow instructions, but it went against her grain. I was driving a cab and I tried to spend every hour I wasn't at work with her, dogging her every move. Truth was, I was scared to death that she wouldn't live long enough to give life to the baby.

Still, we never talked about it. We only planned for the good times when the baby would be with us. There was nothing easy about Teresa's pregnancy, and to be honest, she didn't do any-thing to help it. Even though she was always concerned about the baby's welfare, she somehow felt as though her own welfare had nothing to do with that. She continued to abuse her health and failed to take good care of herself and her hated disease, which much of the time she tried to pretend she didn't have. On top of that, she had kidney problems, and I suppose the drinking had not helped her liver or other vital organs either.

We had even spoke to some of the doctors about her having a kidney transplant, but candidates for those have to promise not to drink and to take extremely good care of their health. That sure as heck wasn't Teresa. All through the multiple hospital stays, the diabetic comas, and often during the real fear, from both of us, that neither she nor the baby would make it, we managed somehow to keep on keeping on until the long awaited day finally came. She spent most of the final two months of her pregnancy in the hospital.

And, to tell you the truth, I was afraid that when the time came for the baby to be brought into the world, that the darn hospital might even let us down.

We were in Gainsville, Georgia when the real pains came, and having almost ignored Debbie's labor with Joey, I decided I should hang in with Teresa all I could. God knows, she'd already been through enough to have delivered ten babies.

Then... there she was. All pink with a squished up face and tiny fists that wouldn't open. She was ready for the world, I guess, clenched fists and all. I mean, it was like the dawning of a new day for all of us.

"I want to name her Dawn," Teresa said, and I couldn't have agreed more. She was a whole, fresh, new beginning for us. We both adored her. By the time they came home from the hospital, Teresa was feeling much better and I began to think that there was hope that the three of us might even find some semblance of normalcy in our lives. For a little while then everything seemed to be right on course. We were Mr. and Mrs. Normal.

Didn't stay that way, of course.

Our lives continued to weave in and out of the fast lane. The baby, as wonderful as she was, and as much as we loved her, didn't slow us down much, or change us at all. We still continued to party like we had good sense.

I'm sure if Dawn could have been aware of anything those days, she would have wondered what kind of parents she had chosen, and where was all this insanity going?

The logical thing-for us at that time-was to hit the road again. About the time Dawn turned six months, we both got ramblin' fever. We bought ourselves an RV, an old Dodge Arrow or something like that, and we hit the open road like a band of gypsies. We hit more towns than Willie Nelson and we might have even been having more fun than old Willie, I dunno.

We didn't know for sure how we were going to support ourselves, but I was never one to wonder where my next meal was coming from or if there'd be a roof over my head when night came. The fact that we had a little baby didn't seem to change our overall outlook on life, except for the fact that we didn't take off on a motorcycle anymore. At least we had a rolling home, and it was obvious right from the start that it would be gathering no moss.

At one of the first campgrounds we stopped, a place called Thousand Trails, we found some of the answers as to the direction our lives would be taking. We were sitting out by the side of the RV relaxing in what there was of the Florida evening breeze, when I heard one of the prettiest sounds imaginable.

"Listen Teresa," I said. "What is that?"

She cocked her head to one side and shrugged. "Somebody playing a fiddle I think," she answered. I leaned back in my chair, closed my eyes and let the strains of that old fiddle fill my head.

"I like the way that sounds," I said, then. Teresa nodded. "That's an old tune... I remember hearing it when I was a kid and my Daddy said he heard it when he was little..."

"What is it?"

"Don't remember, just that it's old," she answered. "Fiddlers in the south always play it when they get together. I don't know if it's a folk song or gospel or what. I always thought it sounded sad and happy at the same time, like it was about something beautiful... that maybe died..."

She was right. It did. I jumped up then and started looking for the source of the music. It didn't take long to track down the fiddle and its player. Just a couple of camp spots down from us there was this hippie-looking couple sitting out in front of their trailer with their little boy. The woman smiled as I approached but the man had his eyes closed and was lost in his own world of the music he was making.

"Hidy..." she greeted me. The man opened his eyes and stopped playing to greet me as well.

"No... no... please," I said raising my hand up in his direction. "Don't stop playing. That's why I came over here. I just wanted you to know how much I was enjoying your pretty music..."

A broad smile spread across his weathered face and he motioned for me to sit down as he laid his bow across the well-worn old fiddle again. The sound he was able to bring forth from it was nothing short of magic.

"Is that a church song?" I asked.

He shook his head. "Nope. Don't go to church. Never did much. Don't believe in all that riga-ma-roll. That's Joann's thing. She even thinks they's a god out there somewhere... I know better. I've looked. He ain't there?"

The woman looked a little embarrassed, although I was sure this wasn't the first time she ever heard him publicly express his lack of belief in a Supreme Being. She quickly made apologies for him and asked me to sit down with them.

"This is Dan," she said indicating with a nod toward the fiddle player. "And, I'm Joann. We're glad to make your acquaintance..."

"Gary," I answered quickly. "Gary Shawkey. Glad to meet you too."

"Dan's a little too quick to speak his mind," she said, looking more in his direction than mine. "He knows there's a God out there, and everywhere else... He just ain't found him yet, but he's a looking..."

Dan drew the bow down across the strings and shook his head again.

"I ain't looking for nothin'," he insisted. "I got it all right here." He indicated with a sweep of his hand which included his wife, his young son, his bus and his trusty fiddle.

"Do you have a wife, Mr. Shawkey...?" Joann asked.

"It's Gary," I insisted. "And yes, I do. Her name is Teresa and she's back at the RV with our little girl, Dawn."

"Oh that's wonderful," Joann said. "I hope we can all spend some time together."

There was something about both of them that just opened doors in my mind and probably in my heart as well. This hippie-looking Christian woman and atheist man seemed so well matched and so at peace with the world and each other. I liked them immediately and I knew right away that they would become important in our lives. Fact was, in the first ten minutes I spent with them, I knew they would be significant and most likely friends for a very long time.

My instincts were right on the money.

Now, where Bob Fullerton had taught me every con-game and slight-of-hand trick in the book, Dan taught me how to give good measure to those I did business with. He may have claimed to be an atheist, but he was one of the most honest and most fair men I'd ever come across. He lived the Golden Rule a lot closer than most of the very best people, and certainly better than some of those who claim to be such good Christian folks. As for Joann, there was a serenity about her that was almost indescribable. Her face was one of complete repose and there was seldom, if ever, a frown across it. She spoke with a soft, gentle voice like one at complete peace with herself. Talk about an odd couple, yet one of the most compatible duos I had ever met. At times I was in awe of one or both of them. Best part was that Teresa felt the same way. Since we had traveled around so much, there had been little time to cultivate friendships, especially close ones, but with these two it was just an instant companionship that we had not even realized we needed so much until they were there to fill the need.

Dan showed me how to make a pretty good living on the road sealing driveways and parking lots, and striping parking lots as well. In fact, the living was extremely good. We had very little living expenses except when we felt like living it up, and the money was good we earned for what I came to feel was a job well done. There was a lot to be said for finishing a day's work with the quiet knowledge that you had given the customer his money's worth, and you had made yourself a good piece of change in return. I think that was called doing an honest day's work for an honest day's pay—plus a bonus.

I liked the feeling. I wondered what old Fullerton would say if he could see me striping those parking lots, using good paint and offering the best job possible the way I promised. He would feel as though he had failed me somehow or certainly that I had failed to heed his teachings. I certainly had fallen from the Fullerton grace. I would also have to explain to him that even though the money was good, there would not be any purchase of no Rolex watch anytime soon either.

We traveled around for some time with Dan and Joann, plying our trade and filling our pockets with the rewards. From time to time we'd take different routes, and we also had our own little business with the Indian turquoise jewelry when it was "the thing to have" by people who wouldn't know one piece of work from another, if it was authentic or not, or even care about it's origin. Well, all right, I hadn't forgotten all old Bob had taught me, and the honest day's work for an honest dollar was not quite the phrase I'd use when talking about our Indian jewelry business.

Our ultimate destination was Washington State.

Why there?

Why not?

Actually, there was a little more to it than that. I'd heard from my old friend and classmate, Dave Smith, who had moved out to Washington to a place called Friday Harbor, off the coast of Washington on the San Juan Islands. He had told me he was making a very good living driving for UPS. Told me too, what a fantastic place Friday Harbor was and how I would love it out there.

"How about it, Teresa?" I had said to her when I first heard about it. "Wanna go...?"

She did. I think my influence and my unrestrained sense of adventure had certainly rubbed off on her. The little Georgia Peach who once seemed to be afraid of her own shadow was now an outgoing person ready for almost anything. Adventure had proven to be extremely contagious, and what more exciting adventure could there be than traveling clear across the country in a Dodge RV, selling Indian beads and sealing parking lots on the way to an island paradise. He had even mentioned something about even more money to be made diving for sea urchins, and selling them to the Asian market where they would be served in the best Japanese restaurants as "Uni."

"Can you think of anything more exciting than that?" Dan asked.

I couldn't.

When I say that the San Juan Islands were a paradise, I wasn't far off. It was one of the most beautiful places I'd ever seen, and I think Teresa fell in love with it too, at least at first. Dave was tickled to death to see us, and in no time at all the diving team of Shawkey and Smith was doing a great business. It was also one of the most amazing things, diving down into the beautiful, clear, blue water for 50-60-100 feet, and the money was fantastic. I had, once again in my life, hit the Mother Lode.

There was however, just a tiny bit of trouble in Paradise.

Dave and I had to travel up and down the coast quite a bit, and Teresa found herself more and more alone. The island, which had once been a wonderful retreat, like a living vacation, was beginning to wear a little thin. She didn't complain much, but the more I was gone, and the more money I made, the more she spent, both on baby-sitters for Dawn and joining the continual parties that went on in the islands.

Then, I drowned.

Oh well, end of this story, huh. Not quite of course. Some of it is still hazy in my mind, but I do recall being down about 70 feet and suddenly there was no air coming through my line. Instead, I could feel myself sucking in vast amounts of water. I could feel myself moving into a dark area where something sat on my chest like a two-ton weight. I gasped for breath, but there was nothing but water. A deep heaviness covered me, and I faintly remember reaching for the buckle on my weight belt. I don't remember undoing it, but obviously I did. I recalled little else except being what I honestly felt was "gone." It was as though there was nothing of me, that I was floating somewhere out there, and even the water had disappeared, yet I was still floating.

Gone.

"Son-of-a-gun...!" Somebody was beating the heck out of me. I was lying on the hard surface of the boat floor. My chest was being heaved up and down and some fool was sitting on me trying to bring me back to whatever the thing called life was.

I started coughing up the sea water and I was never so sick in my life. I was aware of people all around me, excited and concerned voices, with a lot of movement to get the boat back to shore and me to the closest hospital.

"He's alive. He's breathing…"

During the transportation, I kept weaving in and out of consciousness, seeing all kinds of things, all kinds of people, strange faces working over me and a lot of yelling and running. Once, I even made out the words of someone who expressed the sad opinion that I wasn't going to make it.

Well, crap on you, mister. I am too gonna make it.

And, I did.

I was not without residual effects, however. I ended up with a severe case of the bends and nobody had to tell me that my diving career was òver, that my big ship may have finally come in, but I was too busy at the hospital having my darn life saved to collect any of the dividends. No more diving for sea urchins. No more big bucks. Finished. Kaput.

All right, not finished completely. Dave and I went to work with one of the buyers of the little sea urchins, a Mr. Sung J. Kim, of the Sung Fish Company. Sung, a Korean, had his main operations in Vancouver, where he had his fish factory filled with poor, illegal, Asians who worked for zip and made Mr. Sung one of the richest men in the area, and perhaps in all of Korea as well. He actually cut a partnership with Dave and me and we became his official sea urchin buyers all over the west coast, and the Canadian coast as well.

"You will be handling lots and lots of money…" he told us at the onset. "That is why I want to include you in part of the business. You are not likely to steal from your own business…"

Well, thanks for the vote of confidence.

"Is this a deal?" He had asked us the day we began work for him, and we had all three shaken hands on it.

He could not seem to resist adding, as we left on our first sales trip, that nobody got away with cheating him. We assured him that was the farthest things from our minds, and notwithstanding the teachings of old Fullerton, it actually was.

Once again, the money rolled in (and out) and life was a beach. Actually, not quite a beach, and certainly no piece of cake either. But, hey, I was making thousands and thousands of dollars and it felt good. The more I worked, the more money I made. The more money I made, the more Teresa spent and the farther apart we became—not only mileage distance because I was on the road-and water so much—but even when I came back to the island, and in spite of all the things I'd buy for her and how pretty the place was where we lived, there was a growing gap I could not seem to fill. I guess it was called "being there", and I sure as heck was not present that much of the time.

Still, the job, and the partnership with Sung, was just too good to give up. Dave and I had it figured out that in no time at all we could achieve that millionaire status so many people strive for. We were well on our way and Sung was extremely pleased with our work

Until...

I don't know what was wrong with our heads, but neither of us gave it a thought when we hopped out of the car at one of the upscale restaurants on the coast of southern Washington. We were hungry I guess, and full of our own self-importance because we had pulled off some extremely lucrative deals on this particular trip. Our egos and our briefcases were bursting at the seams.

Neither of us gave any thought to our "thoughtlessness" as we devoured big t-bone steaks and talked about the next day's work. Things could not have been going better had we been in charge of "the way things are" ourselves.

As we were walking back out to the parking lot, I felt a rather unusual sensation of something being wrong.

Dave even noticed I had a strange look on my face and asked what the matter was.

"Nothing," I assured him. Nothing that I could think of anyway.

As soon as we reached the car, I think it hit us both at the same time. The window on the passenger side was smashed. I could feel my heart threatening to stop.

The briefcase which contained all the money-a bulging amount of cash—that belonged to the company—to Sung, was nowhere to be seen. It was extremely gone. Thousands and thousands of unaccounted for and untraceable dollars had simply disappeared.

"Nobody gets away with cheating Sung..."

To say we were up the proverbial shit creek without a paddle-or even a boat at this point—would be a kind and gentle way of putting it. One of the first things I did was call Teresa and tell her to start selling our things, and packing what she could, that we would be leaving as soon as I got back.

"What happened?" she asked, and I could tell that she had been drinking pretty heavy.

"Is Dawn okay...?" I asked.

"She's fine... I asked you what happened..."

"Too much to go into on the phone... I'll tell you when I see you... Just sell the stuff and get what you can so we can get out fast..."

"Gary, what in the heck have you done...?"

"Nothin' Teresa... I ain't done nothin'... it's just that something has happened..."

"What...?"

I all but hung up on her and got back in the car with Dave for the dreaded trip back to Vancouver.

"He's never gonna believe that money got stolen..." Dave began as I pulled the car out on the road and headed north. I shook my head.

"No, he won't... no more than I'd believe him if the situation was reversed," I said.

"Darn! What were we thinking, leaving all that money in the car?" Dave slapped the dashboard as he spat out the words in self-disgust.

"I dunno..." I said. "But you can bet that old Sung will think we were thinking of our own pockets... count on it..."

I was right, of course.

We had expected a huge scene, threats, and God knows what else when we arrived back at the main office of Sung Fish Company in Vancouver to tell our amazing story. However, like the inscrutable Asian that he was, Sung simply sat behind his desk and studied both of us for an indeterminable number of seconds or even minutes.

Finally, taking a deep breath and putting his hands on his desk and in almost a whisper asked—actually told—us to get out of his office and out of his sight.

There was nothing I wanted to do more and I even wanted to assure him of that fact, but seeing the stern gaze he leveled in mine and Dave's direction, I thought it best not to say one single word. Goodbye might have even tipped the scales right over the edge. A handshake was certainly out of the question.

I don't mind telling you that both Dave and I spent more than our share of time looking back over our shoulders for many moons to come.

In less than 48 hours all four of us: Dave, me, Teresa and the baby, were on the road to Kissimmee, Florida where we would proceed to start all over once more. Me, back to driving a flippin' cab, coming home to a dinky little apartment that was a far cry from the paradise we had left. Teresa seemed more distant than ever. Even though she had gotten rid of most of our possessions at a reasonably good price and had taken what money we had saved out of the bank, I knew it wasn't going to last us long. I couldn't help but think of the stacks of money that was in those briefcases. If we had taken it, the way Sung believed we had, we would have been in a heck of a lot better financial condition.

But, then I remembered how Joann used to talk about "ill-gotten gain" and some quotes she would offer from the good book, and I felt better that we had been falsely accused.

But gosh darn, that was a whole lot of money...

The marriage did not get any better back in Florida. We fought about whatever the topic of the day was and it was mostly money. I continued to haul passengers from point A to point B in the cab while Teresa drank all the bars dry and partied until the early hours of the morning. I think I was showing my anger and discontent by eating like there was no tomorrow. I was gaining weight like a man on a mission to break the scales. Worse yet, most of the time I didn't even care. It was a sure thing that no Herbalife pills would have helped me in my state of mind.

One night after a particularly bad fight, I did what any angry husband would do. I drove the cab to the train station, bought a ticket to Seattle, Washington, got on and settled back for a three-day cross-country train ride.

Once there, I knew there was nothing I wanted to see or do, so I called home.

"Where are you, Gary?"

"Washington?"

"What in the heck..."

"Nothin' Teresa... I just came here," I said wearily into the receiver. "I'm getting a plane home tonight..."

Silence on the other end. I came back anyway. When I arrived back at the house, things were no different. No worse, certainly no better. It was only a couple of days then until Teresa announced that she was going to Washington state, back to Friday Harbor to visit with some of her old friends. She missed them, she said. I didn't know if she was trying to "get even" or if she simply needed the trip. Either way, I knew she was going to go and I don't suppose I would have stopped her if I could.

Dawn would stay with me, she decided. I could get a sitter for when I was working nights, and it would be better than dragging her all over the country. I agreed.

Two days after she arrived in Friday Harbor, I got a phone call.

"Gary..." she began, and her voice sounded so strange at first that I wasn't sure it was her. "Gary, I'm not coming home... I'm not coming back to Florida..."

I started to say something about coming out there but she was ahead of me. She explained over 2,500 miles of bad phone wire that she didn't just go back out there to see 'friends,' she went to see the man with whom she had been having an affair while we lived out there.

She loved him. Not me.

"You were gone so much, Gary..." she began, her voice sounding both apologetic and accusatory at the same time.

"I know, baby... but... and what about Dawn...?"

"We'll talk later about Dawn... is she all right...?"

"She misses her derned mother..."

"And I miss her too..."

"Hell, Teresa, I miss you... Ain't there something we can do about this crap?"

"No, Gary there's not..."

Every time she called, I'd beg her to come back, and every time she'd say no. I'd even ask how she was feeling, was she taking care of herself and all that. She had started on Prozac shortly before she left and I was concerned about that, but she insisted she was able to make her own decisions, live her own life. She may have stopped being my wife, but I sure as heck couldn't stop being her husband.

I was worried sick about her.

It was six long, miserable months before I heard a soft knock on the door of the apartment late one afternoon, and there she stood. She was even wearing just a little bit of that same sweet grin I'd fallen in love with. I can honestly say that I was never so glad to see anyone in my entire life.

I tried to tell myself the nightmare was over and as I took her in my arms, I honestly made myself believe it, if only for that night. The cold light of morning however, has a way of putting a lot of things in their proper perspective.

Love, as it turned out, did not conquer all. It did not even begin to. We made love that night. No, change that. We made sex. Love didn't have nothing to do with what we did, and to be honest it wasn't even great sex. We were sure as heck not together, that was for darn sure. She was back. She was in our bed again, but together? No way Jose.

A few days later, in some kind of fool desperation I guess, I went out and bought her a snazzy little white Camaro, remembering I suppose, the last time, and how a cute car seemed to work magic. But unfortunately, the magic wasn't in the car, and it bloody well wasn't in us anymore either.

The Sixth Chapter

The Night
The Lights
Got Dimmer In Georgia

"Pale death approaches with an equal step,
and knocks indiscriminately at the door of the cot-
tage,
and the portals of the palace."
—Horace

Looking at the pile of smashed cigarettes on the ground of the parking lot, I tried once again to make some sense of it all.

I couldn't.

Thank God I had reached the place where I was almost numb. Unfortunately, not quite numb enough to get rid of all the horrible pain and agony I was feeling, but just enough to manage to pull a few shallow breaths and keep my head above the dark waters which were all the way past my chin and threatening to close right over the top of me.

I knew I was going under for the last time, but at that point I didn't give a darn. There was not enough strength left in me to fight anymore.

No, I wasn't in the ocean, or in any other body of water, as a matter of fact, I was standing in a dirty parking lot, just outside a tiny little cheap by-the-week run-down motel room at I-85 and I-75, in one of Atlanta's not-so-prized neighborhoods. I guarantee you it was not listed among the 'places to go and see' in the city the Yankee General Sherman once burned to the ground. Too bad he couldn't come back and torch this pig sty.

I kept asking how in the heck we got to this place.

I got no answers.

I had been in a lot of situations before in my life where I felt cornered, trapped, even desperate, and I had certainly had more than my share of close calls and end-of-the-line scenarios, but this was the worst choking kind of misery I'd ever known. There was no relief of any kind in sight, for either of us, and certainly any light at the end of the tunnel would have to be a damned freight train. This was, without a doubt, the worst and the lowest I'd ever been. The old joke about reaching up to touch bottom was not in the least bit funny.

Earlier, I had watched my little girl, the spittin' image of her once beautiful mother, as she cried such sobs she could hardly get her breath. She had been crying for what seemed like an eternity. I couldn't believe those little lungs could last much longer, but she showed no signs of slowing down, much less stopping.

I also couldn't believe that four years had passed since her birth. That had been one of the happiest days of our lives. Just finding out that she was coming had been a major event.

I found myself wishing I'd been tougher on Teresa, made her take better care of herself, but somewhere along the line I reached a point where I figured I couldn't stop her, so I just joined her. She seemed determined to live every day like it was her last-which it could very well have been.

Once more, I wished I had made her take better care of herself. Forced her, for goodness sake. Take a page from old Butthole's book and beat the crap out of her if she didn't do like I said. Like that would have made any sense. Sometimes in our quiet moments, we even talked of our future and how we knew we would have to "settle down" sometime, but living in the now was just too good to stop. To use another line from another song, we were rolling downhill like a snowball headed for hell.

"You worry too much..." she said one night after I had been nagging her once again about taking better care of herself. "Hey... lighten up y'all..."

"I may worry too much," I said. "But you don't worry enough..."

"Yes, I do..." she said, her voice so low I could hardly hear her. "I just don't let it rule my life—what there is of it—and you shouldn't either..."

After that, it was hard to argue with her. She had a point, I thought. I knew her Dad worried sick about her and how we were living and I couldn't blame him.

It had been a wild ride, especially the last four or five years. I was beginning to lose count of the days, much less the years. All I knew for sure was that we had reached what people must mean when they refer to "the end of the line."

This was it. Pure and simple. We just couldn't go no further. I couldn't. Poor little Dawn couldn't, and it was for darn sure that woman back there in the motel room who was pounding her head against the wall in agony had already passed that place some time ago.

How had it come to this? Not only had I failed to take care of Teresa, I had been a horrific father for the little girl that had been so important to us. Her mother had cheated her as well, because at the rate she was going, she would be going and leave her permanently this time. Either I had forgotten, or I never knew, how to stop this speeding train of disaster we were all riding on. We could even see that the trestle up ahead was broken and we were speeding right toward the edge, just like in those old Saturday serial movies they used to show.

Chug-chug-chug-chug-chug-chug-chug. No point in even blowing the bloody whistle. We're headed into the canyon.

Not even the hero could save us now. Hey, we didn't even know any heroes, and I sure as crap didn't fit the description of one. As I had sat there in that stifling motel room earlier that night, I had tried to will my muddled brain to sort it all out, but all the lines were crossed, and what meager information that might have been in there was simply not readable.

I had descended—and I had taken the two people I loved most in the world—right down into the pits of hell.

Dear God, what have I done? How did this happen? I had brought them here to this dump of a motel because we had no place else to go. Their agony was all my doing, or at least most of it. I couldn't take the credit or the blame for the diabetes that was slowly eating Teresa away pieces at a time, but all the other crap was my fault and nobody else's. I ought to have been able to do better by them, I kept telling myself, and myself had agreed. I had promised to give Teresa a better life than she had with Butthole. I had promised to make things wonderful for her. And, to my cred-it, for awhile, I had done that. The good times were, in fact, so darned good that it made the bad times seem all that much harder.

All the good times now were like some kind of a fantasy, something I'd just hoped had happened. All the nights on the beach in Daytona; the sleeping out under the stars as we got through each day, all just figments of my imagination. None of those wonderful things could possibly have happened to these people who were now burning in their own private, lower worlds. What had happened to all those sweet times, wild nights and good mornings waking up in each others arms?

Gone. Heck, we were in Atlanta, Gee-A. Gone with the flippin' wind, I guessed.

Who were these people I was remembering? Surely, not the defeated man who stood like a broken statue in a littered parking lot trying not to remember the image of the pale imitation of the woman he had promised to move mountains for. Heck, he could hardly kick molehills now. What made him think he was ever in charge of how to make Teresa happy?

Things had changed—circumstances had piled upon circum-stances until they had surrounded us with total waste and utter devastation. We had run out of options—and luck—if there ever was any such thing.

"Dad... I need more money... Teresa's getting worse..."

"Son, I've got problems of my own... I just can't..."

"You've got to, Dad... We don't have any place else to turn, and time is running out for all three of us..."

"Will $500 help you...?"

"Anything will, Dad... thanks... I swear you'll get it all back and more... I swear..."

I meant it at the time, but I know he never figured on seeing a dime of the money he kept wiring to me. I don't know how he put up with me for so long. I honestly don't know how he stood it.

After Teresa had come back from her trip to Washington, nothing was ever quite the same. Even her health seemed to deteriorate faster. I will give her credit: she tried. She tried to make things back the way they were, and I tried, too. I wanted so badly to have what we once had together that I would have done almost anything to make it happen.

Nothing helped much. Strangely enough, we had developed another side to our relationship in the time that followed. We became almost soul mates on a journey neither of us really wanted to make, but we didn't seem to have much of a choice. I think I began to see her as a friend who needed help, and I think she began to look at me as a friend who might provide that help.

We clung to each other, not in passionate love, but in a mutual need to be comforted, to know that another warm, breathing body was next to you in the long terrible night. I knew we still loved each other. There was no question in my mind about that, even after all we'd been through, together—and apart. Only now, the love was a different kind of an attachment, one born of absolute need and a fear of a gathering darkness that neither of us wanted to face, or even put into words.

Not too long after our return from Washington was when I got the news that my Mom had died. I made the quick trip to Ohio, but all the time I was gone, I had this awful foreboding that something might go wrong with Teresa, or even Dawn. I was getting paranoid about more things going wrong. God knows, so many things had. Her health had deteriorated to the point where I would end up often carrying her unconscious to the hospital, still afraid they might not even admit her. Sometimes, she would get to stay a few days, and for a few days after she was released, she would show signs of being her old self again. I never gave up hoping that one day she would really return to me: whole, healthy and even free of whatever she felt for the man in Washington or any of the others I suspected she may have spent time with.

I had not been back from my Mom's funeral very long when we got some unexpected company. It was some of the relatives I failed to mention in the Genesis chapter. But, there they were, standing at our front door, bigger'n life. Aunt Charlotte and Uncle Larry had come to town. Aunt Charlotte arrived on the prayer train and Uncle Larry was toting a bible under his arm.

They had come to save the day—and us.

And, yeah, we needed it. We needed anything positive, and Lord I'll have to say that if nothing else, Uncle Larry and Aunt Charlotte were positive as hell, the fire and brimstone kind.

"We'll all go down and hear Brother John Hagee preach," Aunt Charlotte announced on the second day they were there, her voice a notch below shouting. "He's down at Benny Hinn's church in Orlando, a holdin' a revival. He'll preach your troubles away and bring Jesus into your hearts. That's what you need, you know— Jesus in your hearts."

I couldn't argue with that, and neither could Teresa.

"This child needs a healin'," Aunt Charlotte said as she looked at Teresa's frail body and weak countenance. "Yes Lord, she surely does..."

"Amen..." Uncle Larry said.

I couldn't help but wonder what my friend, ol fiddlin' Dan, would think of these relatives.

The crowd was large at the revival and the spirit was high. The good brethren preached one fine sermon. Told us all what we needed in our lives and how we could get it. It sounded so good, so simple, so right and so easy; I wondered why I hadn't thought of it myself. Aunt Charlotte and Uncle Larry were as close to the pearly gates as one could get this side of the heavenly place, just being in the same building with the great preacher Hagee out of San Antonio, Texas.

When they asked for people to come up to be saved or healed, Teresa and I went; followed closely by Aunt Charlotte and Uncle Larry, both praying every step of the long trek down the aisle.

They told us we were saved, and that Teresa would be healed. Caught up in the spirit and excitement of it all, I figured they must know what they were talking about. Life, for a day or two, did seem a lot better. Then reality set in. Even though I had already agreed with Uncle Larry that we should move to San Antonio to be closer to Bro. Hagee's church, I wasn't sure this was what I wanted to do. In my rather weakened state, however, and certainly Teresa in hers, we went ahead and went through with it. We packed up and moved to San Antonio.

God is good.

We were not so good, however.

I don't think what they said we "got," was what people "get" when they have a spiritual awakening, or a new relationship with God. I think what we got was a little bit fooled by all the big to-do, along with Uncle Larry's insistence that he knew the spirit of the Lord when he felt it, and Aunt Charlotte's shouting that her prayers had indeed, glory-to-God, been answered.

Something bigger than Uncle Larry and Aunt Charlotte told me my heart still was not right and it was something I would have to settle strictly between me and God with nobody else, not even the Reverend Brother Hagee, or the illustrious Benny Hinn, with his strange looking hair. I figured it didn't take a rocket scientist, or a television evangelist, to announce when somebody gets saved. That has to be something you experience inside your own heart, and I just didn't think we quite got through that night. At least, I didn't, but I have to hope with all my heart that Teresa did.

You won't be surprised to discover that once I made the move to Texas, I was soon working at another Shoney's, as a manager once again. I even had an asphalt business on the side. Funny, I had done both of these jobs to death and I knew I didn't like either one, but for some strange reason I would go back and let them show me once again what it was I didn't want to do with my life.

I quit. Again. I also quit going to Bro. John's church. I had become disenchanted and disappointed, both in myself and the church, and ending up in San Antonio, where I also did not want to be. God had blessed us however by removing the painful thorn of Uncle Larry and Aunt Charlotte from our sides, but overall we were not doing well at all, not in any way. Teresa was of course, far from being healed.

Another old friend showed up then, this one in the form of my old job as an Herbalife dealer. I jumped back into the Herbalife business with the zeal of an evangelist—I'd taken a lot of notes about how they operated—and before long I was once again doing extremely well. I was not only anxious to get back into it to make money, and because I believed in the product, but I had continued to gain weight to the point where I was miserable. I knew Herbalife would help get me back on the track to losing some weight.

Another thing I had not even realized at that point in my life was that I defined myself by my work. If I was happy in my work, doing something I knew I was good at, and bringing home the monetary rewards for another job well done, then I was happier. Work that I enjoyed gave me a sense of value and worth I could not get anywhere else, nor from anybody else.

One of the first things on the docket after I returned to Herbalife was a large convention of about 30,000 distributors, which was being held in Orlando, Florida. We not only went to the convention, we took our things with us, leaving good old San Antonio for good.

I still wanted my Teresa back, my old smiling, laughing, wonderful Teresa who used to be the center of my existence. In addition to everything else, her kidneys were beginning to fail on her and they started dialysis, first at the hospital, then a sort of do-it-yourself kit that I figured they gave those patients they didn't want to fool with.

"I don't want to use this crap..." Teresa said the first time she saw all the necessary tubes and equipment. I couldn't blame her. I wouldn't have wanted to use it either, but in time it became necessary for her to do it simply to stay alive-if what she was doing could actually pass as living. We managed to get her on a kidney transplant list, but neither of us had much hope of her being called.

I remember one night she simply ripped all the dialysis stuff out and screamed that she'd rather be dead than to live like that. I tried to offer some comfort, but she was extremely upset and in constant pain.

"They're not going to give me no new kidney, Gary," she cried both in pain and anger. "I'm not one of the biggies at the top of the list. They don't give a royal crap if I live or die... and frankly, I don't either."

"Teresa... please don't talk like that," I begged. "Don't even think like that."

"Well," she said in an accusing voice. "Would you put up with this...? Tell me, would you?"

I told her I would, but I wasn't sure I would, and she knew I wasn't sure. I tried to reassure her again and again about the kidney transplant, but she had lost hope that it would ever happen. With the loss of hope went even more of her strength.

In no time, I got the Atlanta area as a Herbalife dealer, so there we went, back on the road to Atlanta again, almost back to the point where we started out.

The night we celebrated Dawn's third birthday was one of our better times. I even grasped at some new hope that things might get even better.

Unfortunately, for Teresa, things got progressively worse health-wise and each day proved to be an even bigger challenge than the day before, just for her to get through it.

The sicker she got, the more time I spent with her, and of course, the more time spent with her meant less time working the Herbalife products, until I reached the place where I was not making any money at all, and we were totally dependent upon handouts from my father and/or anybody else I could get to come to our aid.

We were, to say the least, desperate. We would rent a cheap motel room and leave in the middle of the night, or sneak into one someone had checked out of just to get a few winks of sleep. Sometimes, I stole food.

We spent our days trying one charity hospital after another, trying without success to get some help for her. I had done everything short of standing on a street corner with a sign saying, "Will work for medical treatment," and I would have done that if I had thought it would have done any good.

"Sorry, there's nothing we can do..."

"Has she been drinking?"

"You'll have to come back tomorrow when you can speak to a social worker..."

"Has she been taking her insulin?"

"What's she on...?"

I wanted to scream from the top of my lungs that it didn't matter whether she'd been doing all those things or not, that she was a human being for God's sake, a human being who was barely above crawling and one whose pain was so intense she could hardly speak her own name.

Any port in a storm, I remembered thinking, after we left one particular hospital after having been treated like so much garbage that floated in off the mean streets of this fine, historic, old, southern city.

They say money can't buy happiness, but darnit, it would sure as heck could have bought Teresa some pain killers, and maybe some kindly old Dr. Welby type who might have been able to pull her through once more, or even some nice clean hospital bed with soft sheets where she could at least rest until they could make the pain go away for a little while anyway. It was for sure the head-banging was not going to do it, but it was the only blessed thing she had left.

Money was, of course, in short supply. It was in fact, in no supply. I didn't have to reach into my pocket to count out the last few pieces of coins that rattled at the bottom to know we were destitute as well as desperate. Furthermore, we had already been to all the wells we'd drawn from before and there was no more left for us. It was one dry hole after another. I had almost broken my father more than once, and used up every friend I'd ever had. You can only take everything from somebody once or twice, before they wise up and tell you to buzz off.

Most of them had done just that, and I couldn't blame them. I wouldn't have put up with me nearly that long.

Even though I had always had the "big dreams" of getting rich, as I have said, money itself had never been my goal. Still, standing out in the parking lot that awful night, I thought about how I had sat on the edge of the bed earlier and looked down at Teresa on her hands and knees on the filthy carpet of the miserable room, and it was all I could do to keep from screaming at the top of my lungs. I knew if we had been wealthy citizens of Atlanta, she would be getting the best of care, by the best medical personnel, in the best hospital around.

"Baby..." I half-whispered, even though I knew she was past hearing me. "I never wanted it to be like this for us... how in the heck... did I screw things up so bad?"

Behind me, Dawn leaned her taunt little body back against the plastic headboard and provided the scream I didn't have the courage to let go of. I reached back and lay my hand gently against her little face in hopes of providing at least a little comfort to the child I'd done so little for.

It was an awful thing, dragging this child around from one cheap sleeping room to another, trying to stay one step ahead of whoever was after us for money we owed them for services rendered. Teresa was on Medicaid, but it was never enough, and the fact that she was on it was almost like wearing a big letter on her forehead saying how she wasn't as worthy of treatment as someone with a Blue Cross card or cash money in their pockets.

"Dawn..." I began, but she only cried harder and turned her face away from me. I felt sick at my stomach as I tried once more just to look in her direction.

"Dawn..." I spoke her name again, but her eyes were fixed on her mother on the floor who was still performing the only ritual she had left.

Sure, feel sorry for yourself, Gary.

You're not the one who is in such torment that you're banging your head against the wall.

You're not the one with the tube hanging out of your belly so you can put yourself through all the crap of do-it-yourself dialysis four times a day.

You're not the one who is so darned sick you can't even stand up.

You only have to watch the woman you love more than anything on earth go through all the torture of trying to stay alive when there is little or no incentive to keep on going. I had long passed the place where I was of any comfort or benefit to her. Sometimes I even blamed her because of all our pain, hers, mine, and most pitifully, Dawn's.

"You should take better care of yourself..." I had screamed at her again and again, and even on this horrendous night I reminded her that I had "told her so."

"Didn't I tell you how you would be sorry you didn't listen to me?"

There was no answer, just the horrible rhythm of her thin and weakened body rocking back and forth as she continued to slam the top of her head against the wall again and again. She wasn't even crying any more. Her face was simply a mask of tortured humanity, not hearing or certainly not caring what I said.

Dawn's cries continued to punctuate the small, musty smelling room.

"Didn't I tell you if you didn't take care of yourself... this would happen..." I almost shouted at her.

No response. At least not one directed at me.

"Dawn honey..." I turned around in her direction. "Can you please, God...stop cryin' just for a little while? It hurts Daddy when you cry like that..."

She didn't seem to hear me either. Four-year olds have a way of tuning out those people they'd rather not hear, and it was for darned sure the child did not want to hear my empty words. I didn't blame her. My words were useless... and so was I.

This beautiful child, I thought to myself, had done nothing to deserve such anguish and grief, whereas I probably had it all coming and more. Even Teresa, who had been my sweet Georgia peach, was not even recognizable as the beautiful young woman who had so sweetly greeted me that wonderful spring morning at Shoney's so doggone long ago.

"Could I help you, sir?"

"In every way, sweet thing... in every way..."

I had promised her life would be better. And, it was. I promised I would take care of her forever, that I would never let anything bad ever happen to her again.

Once more, I had lied.

And now, we had come to this.

When I heard some strange, high-pitched, whimpering cries, like that of a small wounded animal, I had looked around the room. At first I didn't know where it was coming from and when I discovered it was originating somewhere deep in Teresa's throat, it cut through my heart like a butcher knife. I was surprised it kept beating, but unfortunately for me, it thumped right on.

Instead of taking her in my arms to offer comfort as I had during those early days, I managed to get to my feet and take a few stumbling steps to the door, where I all but ran through it.

Even when I could no longer hear the screams of my daughter, I could hear those tiny high-pitched sounds of pure agony from Teresa as they seemed to echo through the night sky of Atlanta.

As I stood, almost reeling back and forth in the trash-filled parking lot that night, I wondered how in the name of all that was holy, could Teresa still survive another hour, another minute. How could she hang onto a life that was literally killing her inch by inch, second by second?

I wasn't sure I could. I wasn't even sure I could gather up enough courage to go back to the room again.

It had all started out to be so wonderful.

I tried not to even remember those early days when we were together. It made everything seem so much worse, but I couldn't help it. Everything had been so right. I know we loved each other deeply and sincerely. It was hard to tell where one of us left off and the other began. We both seemed to fill the empty spaces the other one lacked and with each new morning, I loved her more.

It was almost daylight before I finally got up enough strength to go back into the room. Dawn, thank God, had fallen asleep, still sitting up with her little head pushed up against the headboard, her face crusted with the dried tears. Teresa was still on the floor, but mercifully, she was somewhat quieter. She had stopped rocking, and was rolled tightly into an upright fetal position where she appeared to be getting a little bit of fitful sleep. I lay down on the edge of the bed and put my hand gently on her arched back as though I could will what meager strength and life I had left in myself, into her. I reached for Dawn with my other hand trying to connect the three of us together in the only way I knew how.

"Tomorrow, God," I whispered into the now silent room. "Give us tomorrow..."

He did.

The Seventh Chapter

One Day At A Time

"Today is ours: why do we fear?
Today is ours: we have it here
Let's banish bus'ness, banish sorrow:
To the Gods belongs tomorrow."
—Cowley

I t was something I had not been sure I'd ever see again. I opened my eyes to find Teresa studying my face closely, and she was smiling. Not just a little grin, but a big, broad-toothed, shining smile that just lit up the dreary room. I glanced over my shoulder and Dawn, who had scooted down onto the pillows at the head of the bed sometime during the early morning hours, was still sleeping soundly, her tiny face smeared with dirt and still red from the tears shed the night before.

I looked back at Teresa and she was still smiling. I slid off the bed, down to the floor next to her, and took her in my arms. I couldn't believe how much better she looked.

"You're feeling a lot better?" I asked, but the question had already answered itself. She nodded and put her arms around my waist. I had never been so thankful for anything in my life. After a few wonderful minutes, I held her at arms length, trying to get the full impact of her appearance. Granted, her hair was a mess, all matted down and stuck to her head. Her eyes, while they looked hollow, had a hint of the old sparkle back in them. Her color even looked better as she straightened up her body and jutted her rather defiant chin out in my direction.

"Am I a beauty, or what?" she said, still half-grinning.

"You are..." I assured her as I hugged her again. "You really are..."

"Oh sure..." she said, pushing me away as she touched her hair and rolled her eyes upward toward the ceiling. "I'm a real Miss America... and by the way, what the heck did you do with my crown...?"

"I think you broke the sucker last night when you were butting your head against the wall," I said, still amazed at the difference in her, and even my ability to joke about the horror we had all endured. "You sure you're all right..." I asked, peering close to her face.

"Better'n that," she said giving me a short punch in the stomach. "I'm just a rarin' to go..."

"Where?"

"Well, the first place I want to go... is to a cotton-pickin' beauty shop to get this ugly ol' mop fixed," she said, trying to pull her fingers through her matted hair. "Then I want us to take Dawn and give her a day she won't ever forget... I want us all to have a perfectly wonderful day..." She paused long enough to lean her face closer to mine and added, with a half-whispered, old familiar tease in her voice, "... and a perfectly wonderful night tonight..."

God, give us tomorrow.

"Teresa, I can't begin to tell you how good it is to see you feeling, and looking so much better," I said. "Last night... I thought... I mean... it was awful..."

"I know..." she said, as she got to her feet. "I know, but that was last night. This is today, and if you think I look better now, just wait until you see me later... we got any money"

"There ought to be some money out at the desk this morning..." I said. "Dad said he'd wire some to us..."

"Poor man," Teresa said. "I bet he thinks his boy sure did marry a real dud this time..."

"No, Teresa, he loves you too, and he wants to help all he can... it's just that he don't have unlimited funds, even though that's the way I've spent it so far..."

"I'm so sorry..." she said, leaning over to give me a quick kiss on the edge of my mouth. "I told you at the beginning that you didn't know what you were getting in to..."

"Yes I did, and I wouldn't change a thing...except your suffering..."

"And yours..."

"If you had none, then I'd have none..."

She smiled again, told me how lucky she was to have met me, and how much I had meant to her life. It was easy to see she really meant it. Such small victories warmed my heart and I silently thanked my God for the answer to last night's prayers. Teresa then crawled across the bed to where Dawn was sleeping and caressed her cheek to gently wake her up.

"Sweetie... wake up... Mommy's here..."

Slowly, Dawn's eyes opened, and at first she looked startled, then a wave of relief moved across her face as she reached up and put her arms around Teresa's neck.

"You're well, Mommy!" she cried, her large eyes getting even bigger.

"Yes, baby," Teresa answered. "I'm well, and today is going to be a terrific day..."

"It is already, Mommy..." she said quickly.

"I know it is hon," Teresa said. "But it'll get even better... believe me..."

I sure as heck believed her. I was so full of love for her at that moment that I honestly thought I might actually burst from the joy of her miraculous return into the land of the living.

I don't really remember what the weather was that day. I'm sure it was probably hot. I don't know if it was overcast skies or bright sun, windy or still, fair or threatening. I just know it was one of the most beautiful days I'd ever seen and I was not only glad to be alive, but I was grateful and thankful that Teresa was, and feeling so much better. I almost believed a miracle had taken place.

I went to the office to pick up the money Dad had wired to me and by the time I got back Teresa and Dawn were both ready to go. Teresa had found one of those soft, cute little dresses she looked so great in, and Dawn was washed up and dressed in her best outfit, smiling from ear to ear.

"The first thing we'll do is go across the street and have breakfast," Teresa said. It was good to see her taking charge and actually wanting to do something, even if it was something as simple as making a decision about where to eat breakfast. She also informed me she had already made an appointment at a nearby beauty shop to have her hair washed and set. It's hard to describe what a few simple acts others might take for granted, seemed so special to her at this point. I could only stand and marvel at the changes, the improvement in her health, as well as her overall attitude. I knew her rally might not be as good of an indictor as I thought, or that I was pretending it was, but I couldn't help myself. I didn't want to taint any part of this great day by asking her if she was sure she was going to be all right... If she was sure the pain was gone. We were not even living one day at a time, as far as I was concerned, we were living one hour, maybe even one minute at a time. And, for that exact minute, I was in seventh heaven and I believe she was too.

I know Dawn was.

We all walked out of the motel holding hands like school kids. Dawn switched places from time to time, sometimes on one side, with me in the middle, then on the other, with Teresa in the middle. Most of the time though, she insisted on being in the middle, sometimes lifting both feet off the sidewalk and sometimes giggling out of control as she hung on to both our hands. I think we both realized about the same time how long it had been since we'd heard actual laughter from our child, which was at the same time both joyous and sad. Joyous because of the sweet sound of it and sad because we'd almost forgotten what it sounded like.

In the restaurant, neither of us got a chance to hardly speak to each other at all. Dawn was one long string of words, each one overlapping the other with excitement and plans for the day.

"We'll go to the place where there's animals..." She almost shouted in between bites of her blueberry pancakes.

"The Zoo?" Teresa said. "I think we might be too far from the Zoo, but I tell you what... tomorrow we'll get up very, very, very early and go to Six Flags... would you like that?"

The answer came back in exuberant shouts and almost debilitating hugs for both of us.

"I think the answer is, she does..." I said, shaking my head at the wild child who was running from one side of the table to another. Teresa nodded and agreed, then asked Dawn if she could please sit down and quiet down just until we finished our meal. We had no problem getting her to do as we said. She, just as I, seemed to be so grateful for the "whole new day" we were facing, that she was extremely cooperative and willing to be, and do, whatever she was asked.

"What do you want to do now?" I asked Teresa when we left the restaurant. She pointed to her hair. Dawn and I walked her down the street to the little salon and told her we would be out in the park area when she was finished. Instead of feeling as though we were wasting precious time, I found myself relishing every single minute of the day as my daughter and I passed the time walking around, then sitting on a park bench watching the birds and people. It was amazing how much better everyone looked in the sweet light of morning as compared to the ugliness of the night before. I found myself smiling at strangers who walked by, and more often than not, they actually smiled back. I think our happiness must have shown through to everyone who took the time to even glance in our direction.

"Daddy..." Dawn finally asked. "Is Mommy well now?"

"Mommy feels a lot better this morning," I hedged.

"Yeah, but is she well... you know... and not going to cry badly like she did... and not... die..."

I took a deep and almost painful breath. I wanted with all my heart to tell the child honestly that yes, her mother was well, and there would be no more crying and no, she was not going to die. Instead, I reached over and put my arms around her. Holding her close to me I assured her that her Mommy was doing real well and that as far as I knew she would continue to feel pretty good.

"But is she not going to die now?"

I looked closely into those large trusting eyes which were begging for a positive answer from me. She thought her Daddy could make the world turn faster and cause the sun to shine. She also thought I could make her Mommy better. Mommy had even told her that, and Lord knows, I might have too, I don't remember. There was such a desperate plea for assurance from me about her mother that I could feel her pain connecting directly with mine.

Then, God help me, I promised her that her Mommy would not die.

She believed me. Then later, as I watched the beautiful young woman walking toward us in the brand new hair-do with the pastel colored dress flipping about her tanned, slim legs, I almost believed it too. I couldn't remember when she had looked so great to me. I couldn't remember when her whole attitude had been so positive. Not since before we'd gone to Washington did I remember a time when I felt as close to her as I felt at that particular time and place.

I watched Dawn cover the short distance between her and her approaching mother, marveling again at the wonder of the great feeling that went over me as I watched Teresa reach down and wrap the child in her arms. I ignored the fact that Teresa's arms were barely more than little sticks coming out of her short-sleeved dress and I would not even admit that the eyes, although smiling, were still haunted, and I wondered, only briefly, if she was hiding any residual pain from the night before.

"Hel-lllooo beautiful..." I called out to her as she walked up to me with Dawn clinging to her hand.

"Well, helll-ooo yourself, you good lookin' gentleman you..."

"Wanna go for a walk, little girl?" I said, leering down at her as she raised her face to be kissed. "I got candy..."

"Oh Daddy...where?" Dawn moved over to reach into my pockets.

"Hey, hey..." I said quickly. "I'm just teasin' Mommy..." She moved away from me with a slight face and took Teresa's hand again, then reached for mine.

"I take back what I just said then..." she said, grinning.

"What?"

"I referred to you as a gentleman..." she replied. "What you are, is a real Scalawag...an honest-to-goodness... man of low degree... tryin' to take advantage of a sweet innocent lil ol' girl like myself here..."

"You got it!" I answered. "You've figured me out... finally..."

She leaned closer to me as we walked. I hoped she was doing it to be near me and not just to give herself something to lean on.

We walked for quite some time, sitting down often and drinking in the day as though it were the most important time in our lives. Sometimes, I think now, maybe it might have been.

We didn't plan where we would go, nor did we take any particular direction. After walking for awhile, we went to the car and drove around the city of Atlanta for an hour or so, letting the streets take us where they wanted to. We ended up in some of the better sections of the historic old city. Both Teresa and Dawn looked out the windows of the car at the well-clipped and beautifully landscaped lawns, smooth concrete driveways, and impressive homes. Now and then, they would pick out one they would call "theirs."

"Someday..." Teresa half mumbled under her breath. "I want to live in one of those, and have a big yard for the kids..."

"Kids...?" I said questioningly.

"Of course, 'kids,' plural," she shot back at me in pretended anger. "You don't think I want Dawn to grow up to be a spoiled brat with no brothers and sisters to keep her in line, do you?"

"I did," I protested. "And look how great I turned out." She slapped my shoulder and stated simply that she rested her case. Dawn was too busy eyeballing all the laughing children outside in the "perfect" neighborhood to pay much attention to our banter.

"Didn't your folks want any more kids?" she asked then.

"Why should they?" I came back. "They got perfection the first time!"

Once more, she just shook her head at what she referred to as the 'pitiful person' seated next to her, but she was smiling as she did it. It was great to be having fun talking, laughing and kidding each other again. I slowed the car down to a crawl as I continued to look at her in amazement. It had been so long since I'd seen that almost contented and happy look on her face. It was not only one of relief from pain, but love, sincere joy and wonder of simply being alive, coupled with something I'd almost lost myself, hope.

"Oh look up ahead," she said, pointing to a large two-story brick house with tall pillars at the front. "It's an open house... let's stop and look..."

I pulled into the driveway in the old beater car-the great little Camaro being long gone to the re-po man—and I knew if the real-tor was looking out the window, he or she would know right off that we were in no shape to even consider a down payment on that fine piece of property.

It didn't matter. We went in, the three of us, all still full of spit and vinegar and hope, as we inspected every inch of the place in spite of the fact that the lovely lady inside looked at us as though we were day-old road kill or worse. That didn't matter either. We were enjoying ourselves thoroughly and on our way out the door, I called back to thank the stiff-necked, bee-hived haired lady for the tour. I couldn't help adding that as soon as we sold off some of our beachfront properties in Naples we would be in touch with her. There was even a flicker of curiosity on her face as I closed the door behind us. She wasn't sure whether we were putting her on or not, but since she had, no doubt, been around long enough not to judge a book by its cover, or a potential client by his rather obvious lack of finances, she came to the door and called out after us.

"Mister... uh..."

"Mister Shawkey..." I said as we all turned around to face her directly.

"Mister Shawkey... here is my card," she said, walking toward us. "You may call me when you're ready to deal. This is a lovely home and I'm sure your family would enjoy it."

"We would," I said. "In fact, we already have." I then assured her as I slipped her fancy card into my shirt pocket, that I would not forget her when I decided on what property or properties to buy. She managed a weak smile as she watched us crawl into the old jalopy and pull out of the pristine white driveway, which was now sporting a brand new oil slick smack dab in the middle.

We couldn't help ourselves. We all broke out in an uproarish laugh as we drove away from the clearly agitated sales lady glaring down at the black gold at her feet.

"I love that house, Daddy..." Dawn said then, but Teresa assured her that there were even prettier ones than that one and that someday she would live in a beautiful house and maybe even have a pool.

"Promise?" she said, her eyes widening.

"Why not, little purty?" Teresa answered, her voice amazingly confident as she glanced in my direction.

"Why not, sure 'nuff?" I said, half mocking her thick southern accent.

The whole day went like that. We decided to take in a movie, and even though I can't for the life of me remember what it was, I know it was funny, or at least I know we all laughed until our sides hurt. I have tried to remember what it was since then, but it doesn't matter anyway, because if I saw it today, it would not, in any shape or form, be funny.

We finished off our day with a nice meal in one of the better restaurants. I knew when I looked at the outside of it that it was far beyond our means. MacDonald's was beyond our means, but I still had some money in my pocket and I could tell that both Teresa and Dawn wanted to enjoy one of the nicer dining establishments, so we went in.

It was even nicer than it looked on the outside, and even more expensive, but I didn't care. It took almost all I had left to pay the bill, but we all ate well and hearty. The waiter even treated us as though we could actually afford the meal, perhaps even as though we could have afforded the big house we had looked through earlier. I appreciated that and gave him as generous a tip as I could, which just about depleted the funds I had got from my Dad only that morning.

Someday, so help me God, I promise I'll make it up to you, Dad...

Dawn, the house (or for sure one like it) and even the swimming pool, will be yours someday... I won't forget.

By the time we got back to the motel, all three of us were dragging butt. Teresa started into the bathroom to do her dialysis again and I realized how very tired she looked as she went through the door. Suddenly, I felt guilty that I had not made her rest more;

that I had taken advantage of a good day by pushing her too far, and doing too much, and I hollered my thoughts through the bathroom door. From the other side, she protested, assuring me that she was a big girl and knew her limits better than I did. Dawn was hardly through the door before she headed for the bed. She was asleep almost as quick, but not before she checked again with Teresa about Six Flags when she came out of the bathroom.

"We're going tomorrow... right Mommy?"

"Right, sweet thang..." Teresa came back as she kissed her good night.

For awhile both of us sat on the edge of the bed watching Dawn sleep. What a difference from the night before, I couldn't help thinking, and as though she read my mind, Teresa leaned over and put her arms around me.

"It's all right," she assured me.

"I know," I said, realizing then how exhausted I was.

"Hold me..." she said then, as she pulled my arms around her and lay back on the bed, taking me with her. For the longest time we both lay there, not talking, hardly breathing, each of us lost in our own thoughts, which may have paralleled each others. We did not exchange our fears or our dreams at this particular time.

"I had plans for us tonight..." she began, her voice soft against my neck.

"Same here..." I answered, tightening my arms around her. Then, so she would not have to offer the excuse of being exhausted, which I knew she was, I told her quite honestly, that I was really bushed myself, and as much as I wanted to make love to her, we had overdone everything else this day, and after all, I assured her, there would be another day, and more importantly, another night.

"Yes..." she said in a small voice as she snuggled up closer to me as her eyes closed almost immediately.

"Have fun today?" I asked then, and she assured me in an extremely tired voice that she could not remember ever having a better day in her entire life.

"I'll get you a house like that one someday, Teresa... better even... with that pool for Dawn," I solemnly promised, as I felt her breathing become even and relaxed. She had fallen asleep without even hearing my promise, but it didn't matter because I knew that she knew I would when I could.

I tried to keep awake for as long as I could, savoring the difference between this night and the one before. I don't know how long it was before I drifted off, but I do know that I slept soundly for the first time in months, completely content as the three of us in the one bed, slumbered away the night on the lumpy mattress in the cheap motel in not-so-exclusive section of Atlanta.

When the first light of morning came through the soiled and faded drapes that would not pull together all the way, I looked over at Teresa, who was not moving except for the rhythmic shift of her chest as she breathed in and out. As had been the case for months and even years, I always checked on her much the way a parent will check on a new baby, making sure it is still breathing, and all is well.

I eased out of bed where I had slept between Teresa and Dawn, and as I crawled across Dawn, she opened her eyes.

"Daddy... are we leaving for Six Flags?"

I held my finger to my mouth and indicated my head toward her mother. Dawn glanced at her and made an apologetic face.

"That's OK hon... you and I will go have breakfast, then we'll come back... for Mommy."

"She needs to rest, huh?" Dawn said, far older and more sensitive than most children her age. I nodded.

As we sat in the little Mom and Pop restaurant across the street, I began to feel an uneasiness I had at first denied, but it had been with me ever since I woke up, maybe even before. Slowly, I allowed other small 'facts' to present themselves to my now conscious mind. Teresa had not had to get up all night long. Even though she had managed to take reasonably good care of herself the previous day, giving herself the home-made dialysis at regular intervals, I knew she had not done that at all during the night. At first there was such a feeling of elation thinking that she was so much better she had not had to resort to the hated procedure which tormented her so much. The feeling was short-lived however, and I knew it was not only not a good sign, but a bad one, one I could no longer pretend did not exist.

The growing hot coals in the pit of my stomach became more and more unbearable as I rushed Dawn through her cereal and toast. My bacon and eggs sat half finished on the flowered plate in front of me. My eyes kept going back to the motel window until suddenly I jumped up from the table and taking some wadded up bills from my pocket, I threw them on the table without even counting them or asking how much I owed. I grabbed Dawn by the arm and headed for the front door.

"Daddy... I'm not done with my juice..."

I didn't even respond to her plea.

Running across the street then and half-dragging Dawn, I made it to the door of the motel where I stood almost frozen in my tracks.

I had not even locked the door and as finally I pushed it open, the room seemed to spin around me. I did not have to walk to the bed to know. I did not have to check her pulse, or look close to see if she was breathing. I knew she was not.

Worst of all, Dawn knew it too.

I don't know if my face gave it away, or if I might have even said something, but suddenly the child was screaming as though she would pull her insides out through her little mouth. I remember trying to console her somewhat, at least I think I did, but she kept screaming as she pounded me with her fists and reminded me of my broken promise. I vaguely remember a crowd gathering and someone asking if we needed a doctor and I'm not even sure if I went to the phone to call an ambulance or if someone else at the motel did.

Soon, they came.

The "they" I'm talking about are the people who always come when something like this happens. The flashing lights, the sirens, the men and women with their serious faces and covered gurneys, policemen with their professional voices, pads and pencils. Curious onlookers, pushing for a place in line where they can see what is going on, yet not understanding any more than I did, exactly what the situation was.

They could see, and they could hear the people who came speaking in low tones about the deceased. They knew the thin young woman from the motel room was dead. I knew she was dead. And, the child who was screaming for her mother knew she was dead, even though her father had told her, promised her, that would not happen. Someone tried to help console her, a woman I think, perhaps someone passing by.

I couldn't offer the child any comfort. I was helpless. I had promised to take care of Teresa, promised her, promised Dawn, promised myself... and I had failed.Death had beaten me, just as it had other fools before me, and others who would come after me.

Even more serious than my failing was the simple fact that the suffering child did not understand exactly what being "dead" was. She had no way of knowing that the mother who laughed and walked with her the day before would not ever be doing that again. She could not fathom the fact that they would not "some-day" be moving into a house like they had just seen. They would not look out the tall windows at the aqua colored swimming pool where her brothers and sisters were playing. She did not know that even though we would postpone the trip to Six Flags today, there would be no later day, no other sweet tomorrow, that we would make that wonderful trip together. She did not realize for sure that this was not just another temporary trip to the hospital, or that her loving mother would not return to us as she had in the past, and that we would begin again. She also did not know that her terrible screams, which cut through the thick air of that Georgia morning, sliced through my heart like a jagged rusty blade.

"Over" was another word Dawn did not understand.

I didn't understand it either.

Only Teresa understood.

The Eighth Chapter

An Angel Named Gloria

*E*ven though I know this isn't usually done in an autobiogra-
phy, I have to let my Aunt Gloria tell this chapter. After the
funeral was over, there was a dark haze that seemed to surround
me. I do know I rented a truck to take our things back to Akron,
and I had called Gloria about keeping Dawn. I don't remember
loading the truck, or packing any clothes. I may have just tossed
them into the back of the truck. To my discredit, I can't even
remember how much I told Dawn about what we were doing. I do
recall telling her we were going back to Ohio and that she would
be staying with Aunt Gloria who loved her very much.

I don't even think she answered or even looked directly at me.
I remember the trip only in bits and pieces. We stopped only to go
to the rest room and grab a quick bite to eat. It was as though I
was possessed, that I needed to get out of Georgia as fast as I
could. Foolishly, I thought the more distance I put between us and
the horror we'd been through, the less it would hurt.

I was dead wrong.

There was not much conversation between us. Dawn sat hud-
dled in the corner of the truck cab and I drove like a madman. We
must have had a very busy guardian angel watching over us,
because I was in no shape to do much of that. I think I told some-

one who suggested I get someone to drive us back to Ohio, that I was just fine.

I lied.

When the phone rang, I got one of those feelings you always get when the news is not good. I dropped the last piece of clothing in the washer and ran up the steps to answer the call.

"Aunt Gloria...?"

"What is it, Gary...is Theresa..."

"No," he answered. "But she's dying, Gloria. I don't know if she'll live through the night."

"I'm so sorry...If there's anything I can do..."

"You can," he interrupted. "You can take Dawn for me... As soon as... As soon as..." He was unable to go on but I assured him that there was no question that Dawn could stay with us as long as he needed her to stay.

I was not really Gary's aunt. We were actually cousins. My mother and his mother were sisters, but because of the age difference, Gary had always called me his Aunt, and even as a child he seemed to gravitate to me whenever there was a problem, and even when there was good news too. He always wanted to share his times, both good and bad, with me.

Because Gary was such an amazing character-actually from the first time I ever saw him as baby—I thought he was so special. I had no idea the adoption was not exactly on the up-and-up. I remember how everybody was so excited over the new family

member and I thought he was just the most beautiful little thing
I'd ever seen, with those big eyes that looked right into your heart.
I couldn't stop staring at him, and right from the first he had this
marvelous personality that just reached out to everybody. You
couldn't help but love him. He just stole my heart. He was that
kind of a baby.

"It's so sad," somebody said that first evening we went to see
him and everyone agreed that his terrible situation was indeed
heartbreaking.

"Imagine all that his poor mother and father are going to
miss?" My mother said and my aunt nodded in agreement.

"It was a terrible accident," my aunt said then, her voice taking
a somber tone.

"Both parents killed—the father instantly—and the mother living only long enough to give birth to this wonderful child..."

We all discussed the dreadful tragedy although there was not
much more we knew about it. My aunt said they had received a
call from a priest they knew in New York, who told them about
this poor child in Georgia, and they had rushed out in the middle
of the night to take in this little orphan as their own. I remember
thinking it was like a scene right out of the movies, so dramatic
and tragic, yet from all that pain had come such a miracle for our
family.

They named him Gary and he was a member of our family
from the first moment we all saw him. He also grew to be the
apple of my grandmother's eye, and all through his years of growing up, none of us, including Gary, ever had any reason to doubt
the story told about his birth. It was one of those family stories
that gets passed from one to the other, a little more unusual and

certainly more dramatic than the normal birth story, to be sure. The thing is, we had no idea how much more unusual and really dramatic his birth story really was.

My aunt and uncle raised Gary according to Dr. Spock and all the other books on turning out a healthy, happy child, with one exception. I remember he loved those very-bad-for-you Ho-Ho cupcakes, and in spite of all their health consciousness, they allowed him to fill up on those sugar-filled concoctions all the time. Still, there was very little any of us could deny him because he was such a charmer right from the beginning.

In my wildest dreams I never imagined that child would turn out to be one of those babies that were sold by the infamous Dr. Hicks in Georgia. Even when the big, bold headlines broke the story, it still did not seem real to me because Gary, as far as I was concerned, was one of us, always had been and always would be, and the children they spoke about in that baby-selling scandal was about other children in other places. Even after I heard the news, and knew it to be a fact, it didn't matter to me where Gary came from, or under what circumstances. I think that went for everyone else in the family as well. I wondered why my Aunt had not told us or him about it, but she was a woman who kept to herself a lot, so I figured she thought it was none of our business. By the time we found out about the true story, she had already passed away. Maybe she was embarrassed about the way they got him. Later, I realized she might have been afraid, and rightfully so, that some-one would come and take him away from her. Regardless, Gary was still my special cousin, and in fact, I often referred to him as my "vagabond cousin" because he never stayed in one place long enough to find shade.

It was only a day or two after that first frantic call saying how sick Theresa was, that Gary called again. I don't recall exactly what he said, but he sounded terrible and he mumbled something about leaving right after the funeral.

It was late in the afternoon when the car pulled into the driveway. Gary had driven non-stop from Georgia, and when the two of them walked up to the front door, they were almost unrecognizable. Gary looked as though he had not slept in weeks. His eyes were red rimmed and he looked as though he had not bathed or shaved in days. His hair was uncombed and his eyes mirrored the distress and anguish he had just gone through. Compared to Dawn however, he looked good. I don't think I've ever seen a child look as forlorn and lost as that little four-year old girl did as she stood in my doorway, leaning against her father's leg and clinging to his limp hand. She looked like one of those refuge children you see in war-torn countries on television with dead, dry eyes and no hope for tomorrow. Still, I could almost sense the strength that lay inside this amazing child.

"Dawn... Hello... I'm your Aunt Gloria too," I said, as I knelt down to talk to her. Her eyes did not meet mine, and she didn't say a word. Instead, she moved closer to her father. Gary leaned over and tried to talk to her, telling her that I was his favorite Aunt and that she was going to be staying awhile with me and that he would be back to see her every weekend. Both of us talked to her for some time, but she remained silent. Finally, we went inside and I told Gary to bring her out on the back-screened in porch where we could all relax. I knew they both needed to sit and rest for awhile but Gary was as restless as Dawn was unresponsive. Slowly though, she began to warm up to me a little, allowing me to hug her and even hold her close to me as we sat on the porch settee. I guess she figured if her Daddy liked and trusted me, I must be all right.

Chagrin Falls, Ohio might as well have been Mars as far as the child was concerned. She had lived in the south all of her life and knew nothing of this part of the country, or of us for that matter, except what she'd been told. She had just gone through the trauma of losing her beloved mother and now she was among strangers, and for all she knew, she was losing her father as well.

The Modliszewski household was certainly not a quiet place. We already had a pretty full house, but as my mother used to say, 'There's always room for one more', and there was certainly room for Dawn. My husband, Frank, and I had four children, twins Madaline and Stephanie were still in high school and of course, living at home, Brenda, who was then a freshman in college, and our oldest, Kevin, who was out of school and working. About a year before, my mother-in-law, Pauline, had come to live with us and with her came Marie, her daughter, who was born with Downs Syndrome. She was 40 years old, but had the mentality of a child about seven.

Right away, Marie recognized Dawn as someone who could be her friend. At first, she made several overtures toward Dawn, but Dawn did not respond right away. Looking back, I'm sure, she could not.

Still, that first evening, Gary was restless, and in spite of my pleadings for him to stay longer, he seemed anxious to get moving again. I think he needed to get the good-byes between him and Dawn over as quickly as possible. I was more than a little concerned about him, his state of mind as well as his state of health. He said he was going by his dad's house, and he planned to stay in the area because of Dawn. He was not, he insisted, going back to Florida. I tried to talk to him a little about Teresa, but I could tell that he had simply removed himself from the whole situation. I think it was the only way he could deal with the pain he was feeling. The only thing he told me was that he did all he could, regardless of what they thought.

"Who's they?" I ask.

"Her family..." he said. "They think... they blame me..." I could tell that he was close to falling completely apart so I didn't press the conversation any farther, except to assure him that I knew he had done all he could, because I knew him and I knew how much he loved Teresa.

Before leaving, Gary went out to the back of his car and took out a battered old cardboard box. It was all he could do to hold himself together as he handed it to me. On the top of the box the words, "Things for Dawn," was scribbled across the lid.

"There are things...in there..." he said, his voice breaking, as he nodded toward the box. "Things of... Teresa's... and I thought... Dawn..." He couldn't finish the sentence.

I nodded; thinking how sad it was that this was all the little girl had left of her mother...that, and a host of memories, both good and bad. Even today that old box still sits up in my attic, waiting for the right time when Dawn is old enough to receive this last gift from her mother.

I was bracing for the avalanche of tears from Dawn when her Daddy left, but they did not come. We just sat for a long time on the back porch as I held her close to me and hugged her tightly. I spoke softly to her, trying to steer the conversation away from both Gary and Teresa, but I knew they were both very much on her mind.

I could only imagine what was going on with Gary as he pulled out of the driveway and took off down the street as through he were being chased by the devil himself. If I could, I would have made him stay as well because frankly I thought he might be a danger to himself.

Days passed before Dawn would make any indication that she would adjust to our household. Members of the family all tried to get responses from her, but she had withdrawn into a small shell, and there were times when I was afraid she would never come out. The only hope was that she was responding to me somewhat, sitting for hours at a time, close by my side without saying a single word. I couldn't help but wonder what was going on inside that little head, but from the sadness in her eyes, I wasn't sure I wanted to know for sure.

I remember looking at my new little house guest one day as she sat in the center of the living room floor, slowly rocking herself back and forth, as though in a trance. She would either rock or spin around in circles, with her eyes focused on nothing at all. It was frightening just to look at her and know you could not reach her or touch her inner pain. Even when she would stand, she could not stand still. She had to be moving, as though she wanted to keep ahead of whatever was trying to overtake her.

Dawn looked so much like her mother it was amazing. I had only met Teresa twice, and the last time was when she and Gary came to Ohio for a visit. We all liked her immediately that first time we saw her and I was so pleased to see her again. She was several months pregnant, and one of those sweet southern girls who just stole your heart right away. She looked so delicate and frail, but of course she wasn't. Teresa was probably one of the strongest and most independent people I have ever met. Had she not been strong, she would have been gone long before she did. We had all been told about her illness, how serious it was, and our hearts just went out to her, and to Gary as well. The fact that she was pregnant could not be good for her, I thought, but I knew it was none of my business and in spite of the fact that her health was not great, I thought she had a sparkle in her eyes I had not seen the first time we met. Looking back, I guess it was that special glow that some pregnant women seem to have. If there was ever a woman happy to be pregnant, it certainly was Teresa, regardless of the circumstances.

Something she said that day however, chilled me. Later I told Frank I thought the girl had some kind of a "death wish."

"Why would you say that?" he asked.

"I dunno," I replied. " It was just... I don't know... her attitude. We were talking about the baby, and I said I hoped she got along all right with her pregnancy, and she just shrugged, and said 'I don't care if I die, I'm having this baby...' and went right on with the conversation as though everything was fine."

"Well, I don't see that as a death wish," Frank came back. "A little risky, I guess, but not exactly a death wish."

We had dropped the subject at that time, but sitting on the couch in the living room, watching Dawn moving back and forth, I could almost see her mother's determined face as she spoke about having her baby...no matter what.

I don't care if I die...I'm having this baby.

Dawn managed to get through the first few days without incident, but the nights were something else entirely. Her nightmares were often and violent. She would wake up, screaming loud enough to wake the neighbors a mile away. As soon as I heard the screams, I would hit the floor running to her bed.

"It's all right, baby... it's all right..." I would tell her over and over, as she clung to me as though she was afraid I would leave her, too. I would hold her close, sometimes singing softly, until she would finally stop crying and fall back to sleep. Sometimes she would still be sniffing during her sleep and I would sit on the edge of her bed until I was sure she was back into a deep sleep.

One night, as I crawled back into my own bed, Frank rolled over and asked me how long I thought the nightmares would last. My first thought was 'all her life,' but I told Frank I guessed they would last until she gets over the terrible fear of losing. I wondered, and I'm sure Frank did too, if this was ever going to happen.

Unlike the rest of us, Marie did not seem to be the least bit worried about Dawn. She simply took her at face value and sat close by her most of the time, as though waiting for Dawn to notice her. Dawn did seem to respond more to Marie than the rest of us, but she lived for the weekends when her father would visit. It was only then that there would be a trace of a light in her eyes, but it would disappear as soon as the sound of his car had gone.

On one of Gary's visits, we asked about having legal guardianship so Dawn could be on Frank's insurance. As it was, the child had no kind of insurance and we didn't know what we would do if she became seriously ill. Gary agreed because he always wanted whatever was best for Dawn, and he knew this was best, and it certainly did not mean he was giving up custody. He trusted us that much—to know we would never take Dawn away from him—that we only wanted to protect her, as he did.

One afternoon after she'd been with us a couple of months, I noticed Marie getting out her coloring books and crayons. She had not paid much attention to them since Dawn had come, but I guess she must have gotten bored watching her new little friend without much feedback.

She sat down on the floor next to Dawn, who was watching Sesame Street with Pauline. I think Dawn figured when she

watched television, she did not have to worry about having to
interact with anyone. Losing herself in a world of Muppets was a
way to avoid having to deal with real life, which had been, up
until then, not a lot of fun for this child.

Spreading out the coloring books on the floor, Marie picked up
a red crayon and began to color. She colored carefully, making an
effort to stay well within the lines. We always complimented
Marie on how well she colored and how pretty the pictures were
when she had completed them. She took a lot of pride in her artistic ability but I think she wanted some kind of recognition from
Dawn as well.

Dawn glanced over at her a couple of times. Then, much to my
delight, and Marie's as well, Dawn slowly picked up a green crayon and began to color on the other page. She moved the crayon
erratically and pressed down hard as she paid no attention to the
lines. Quickly, Marie offered her one of the other books. Dawn
took it and selected her own page to color, still moving the
crayons wildly and almost angrily outside the lines and sometimes
off the edge of the page, creating a splash of color without any
semblance of artistic ability. Marie had long since stopped coloring
and watched, with interest and some concern I think, as Dawn
completely colored all over the picture of a beautiful Princess
standing outside a large castle.

Marie motioned for Dawn to watch as she colored a picture of
another princess in a beautiful coach. She carefully moved the
crayons inside the lines and created a childlike masterpiece, leaning back to observe her work and see if Dawn was appreciative as
well.

"Who is that?" Dawn asked.

"The Princess..." Marie replied. Then looking at Dawn, told her it was her.

"You're the beautiful Princess..."

Suddenly, Dawn turned to look at Marie with a look of sadness. Marie then reached over, took Dawn's hand, and laid it down on a new page, and slowly moved the crayon in short gentle strokes inside the lines of a very large bear.

"See... it's easy... if you don't make big marks... easier to keep in the lines," Marie told Dawn, who was beside herself with amazement. Marie slowly removed her hand and once more Dawn began to make wide swipes with the crayon. Again, Marie placed her hand over Dawn's to guide her, admonishing her gently to color very slow and easy, so it would be pretty. For the first few strokes, Dawn did as she was told, but would soon return to her erratic scribbling, only to find her hand slowed down once more by her new friend and mentor.

It was a wonderful thing to watch them. I felt as though I was watching a personal little miracle take place. As the weeks passed, Marie's patience was amazing, and Dawn's progress, although extremely slow, continued. We were all amazed that little by little she was able to keep the colors within the lines. Once Marie had taught her that, she then began to show her the difference in colors. It was a long, painstaking process, this teacher and her student, but the results were magnificent. It was no longer a small miracle; it was a large one, and a wonderful one.

Dawn remained in our house for about a year. After the coloring incident, she began to open up to all of us and became a marvelous addition to our family. With each passing day she grew in strength and the face that I never thought I would see smile again sometimes became even radiant and glowing, especially when her father came to visit. The nightmares almost disappeared and on the rare occasions when they did come, Dawn managed to make them go away on her own.

"Daddy, come and look at the picture I colored," she cried out. "Marie showed me how to color real good..."

"I can see that," Gary said, holding the coloring book up in front of him. "That's very pretty. Could you color me one?"

"I did already," Dawn came back. "That's it..."

Thankfully, I noticed a positive change in Gary as well. The creature that had showed up at my door that warm summer afternoon, looking as though he had gone his last mile, seemed to have reached a new plateau in his life. The sadness was still there in his eyes, but when he walked through the door, Dawn was in his arms in no time and smiles came easier for both of them.

Although I knew life would never be the same for either of them, I felt we had at least passed the crisis.

"You OK?" I asked Gary after a few months, and he assured me that he was. "Thanks to you..." he added, forcing a smile.

"I didn't do anything..."

For a long moment he just looked at me and then slowly shook his head as some of the sadness returned to his eyes.

"You have no idea..." he began, and then hesitated. "You have no earthly idea..."

Life, I had told him from the beginning, goes on, and one day about a year after he had brought Dawn to live with us, he finally agreed with me. I knew he had been getting his life back together with a new business and new friends. I was happy to see the old Gary, looking and acting like himself again. More importantly, I was happy to see life returning to Dawn.

"She's doing pretty good, isn't she?" he said then, looking at Dawn, who was running circles around Marie, whose face was always radiant and smiling when she was with Dawn.

"She's doing wonderful..." I came back. He let out a big sigh and I knew the time would soon come when he would take Dawn to live with him all the time, and even though I knew that was best, it was going to be hard to let her go. It was going to be even harder on Marie to let her go. It was difficult to say which one of them had been more helpful to the other.

"Well, Vagabond," I said, slapping him on the back then and lightening up the mood. "Are you finally going to settle down in one place?"

"I'm always settled in one place," he said, grinning. "One place at a time is all I can occupy."

The Ninth Chapter

Headlines Reveal Secrets

"A secret in his mouth,
Is like a wild bird put into a cage;
Whose door no sooner opens, but 'tis out."
—Jonson

There's nothing like picking up the morning paper and seeing part of your life splashed across the headlines right smack dab in front of you.

Babies sold to Akron Couples during the Sixties

Georgia Doctor Had Local Connections

The dateline said, "McCaysville, Georgia." I looked at the photograph of a birth certificate, with its fancy little edges and unusual writing, and at the bottom, the name of the attending physician leaped out at me like gangbusters. Dr. Thomas J. Hicks was the attending physician on the certificate.

That was my doctor.

McCaysville, Georgia was the place where I was born.

It was also in Georgia that my birth parents had met with a tragic accident which left me an orphan.

My parents had never kept my adoption a secret from me. As early as I could remember, they had openly discussed my origin, or at least part of it, even the fact that I was born in a small town in Georgia. My legal-looking birth certificate was filled out as though my adoptive parents were my birth parents and was signed by Dr. Hicks. It had never been a big deal to me that I was adopted. I felt fortunate to have good parents, and even though they had flaws and shortcomings like any other parent, they were still my very own parents. I figured if they could love me, even if I wasn't perfect, then surely I could return the favor.

The news story hit, strangely enough, on Mother's Day in 1997.

At first, I picked up the phone to call my Dad, then decided to drive by his house and talk to him. It wasn't that I wanted to confront him about this matter, nor did I intend to berate him in any way about not being told about this. I was not as upset or unraveled, as I found out later, as many of the others were. We were also to learn that this kindly old country Doctor sold more than 200 babies to desperate people in the 50's and 60's. Each baby came with one of the fancy, falsified birth certificate like they showed in the newspaper, so no one could trace the child to his or her mother.

I remember that sometime after my Mother's death, Dad had mentioned to me one day that my birth mother might still be alive. If I had thought about it all, I might have guessed that, but frankly, it had been of little concern to me one way or another. I think I told him just that. The truth was, I had a life. I was living it, by this time, very well. I had never been one of those "adoptees" who kept agonizing about "finding myself" or "knowing my roots", even though I felt a lot of sympathy for those who couldn't seem to get on with their lives until they had all the loose ends tied up. Heck, I had already found myself several times, and as far as my roots, I suspected, perhaps rather crudely, that maybe we should just let sleeping dogs lie.

Later, when I got to know some of the other "Hicks Babies" in the Akron area, I had a certain amount of compassion for their search for more knowledge of what happened, but it did not shake my world the way it did some of the "babies". I did know for a certainty, however, that May morning as I pulled into the driveway at my Dad's, that I was one of the infamous "Hicks babies," and I also knew that those of us who had been the main attraction during those human transactions were in for a wild ride.

I just didn't know how wild it would get.

"See the paper, Dad?" I asked when I walked through the door. He nodded.

"Is that our Doctor Hicks?" He nodded again.

"Why didn't you ever tell me about this?" I asked, trying to make sure he knew I was neither accusing nor condemning him for what had happened more than 30 years before.

"Your mother...didn't want us to ever talk about it..." he said slowly, and I could tell it was painful for him to speak of it even then.

"Yeah, but Dad, both of you know it didn't matter to me," I assured him, as I sat down next to him. "You and Mom were the only parents I ever had...ever wanted. I'm not mad or even upset that I didn't know the whole story. You didn't have to worry about what I would think, and there was no reason to make up the story about my birth parents being killed in a car wreck..."

"Your mother..." he began again, and I could tell he was still uncomfortable about it and I decided there was no reason to put him through any more anguish when it was of such little importance to me.

"It's all right, Dad," I reassured him again. "I was just curious, honest. That's all. I hope you know that as far as I'm concerned it's really no big deal."

As it turned out however, it was a "big deal" to more than one person, if not to me.

It had all started when Jane Blasio of nearby Jackson Township uncovered some of the long-hidden secrets in her quest to find out more about her heritage. Even though I did not share that need to unravel any kind of mystery about my past, I came to understand Jane and her need to pursue it. After getting to know her, I found myself wishing we'd discover we were brother and sister, and later there were even some DNA tests done, but nothing has proven to be conclusive. Several of the children did find out later that they had brothers and/or sisters living in the area, and in other places, and that sounded good to me. I had always been an only child and the thought of having siblings appealed to me, even more than finding the woman who gave birth to me.

Jane was one of those who wondered about the woman who brought her into the world, wondered if she loved her, why she gave her up, and all those nagging questions that some adopted kids seem to have. She knew that her adoptive father, who was dead by the time this news broke, bought two babies after an Akron woman had spread the word about a clinic in a remote

Georgia town. People could buy a baby there, she told them, without any red tape or questions asked—for about $1,000.

She discovered that about 49 couples in the Akron area bought babies from Dr. Hicks, who delivered most of the babies in that small town in Georgia. On one hand he was the kindly old country doctor, and on the other, he performed illegal abortions and sold babies as a sideline.

Of course, he didn't keep any records, and when he died at age 83 in 1972, he didn't leave much behind, except whispers and rumors—nothing on paper. That was the main reason Jane decided to go public with the story. She hoped that there might be other adoptees' that would come forward, and maybe even someone who knew more about the story could fill in some of the blanks.

I don't think she had any idea as to the can of worms that would be opened. It was like a bomb exploded. After the story appeared in the Beacon Journal, more than 300 people called Jane. The woman who had been helping her in her search (Linda Davis, Fannin County Probate Judge) was also overrun with phone calls. They had been compiling a registry called "Silent Legacy" to match birth mothers with their families.

Before the end of the following day, both Akron and McCaysville, Georgia were overrun with television crews, reporters and curiosity seekers, all wanting to know more about what went on thirty to forty years before. USA Today was on hand, both in Georgia and in the Akron area as well. It was also discovered that children had been sold to couples in Tennessee, Virginia, New Mexico, Illinois, Indiana, Florida and Georgia, as well as Ohio. Talk show producers were on the phone, and movie producers in New York, and tabloid journalists, both American and foreign, were flocking down like a bunch of birds on road kill. There were all kinds of stories, some half-truths, others outright fabrications, that swirled around everything, and poor Jane, as well as some of the others, found themselves right in the middle of it all. All Jane had wanted was to find a link to her past, and here the whole Pandora's Box had been unsealed and there was no way of getting that lid back on again.

There were rumors of hidden birth records and the judge in McCaysville even ordered the local sheriff to open the Hicks' family mausoleum. It was empty. By the end of June however, there had been a match of three birth mothers and their children.

There were some happy stories, but there were many sad ones as well. I will admit that I was curious enough to call the court house in McCaysville, but I hit a dead end. During all the time everything was going on, I only heard a rumor, one of those 'somebody said that they knew somebody who thought maybe it was possible' that I had a brother.

"Good," I thought. "Now he can buy me a birthday present and Christmas present for every year he missed, and I'll really be rolling in gifts." When someone mentioned that I would owe him an equal number of gifts, I laughed and told them that because I was the "little brother", I could not be expected to get anything for him. I know some of the others looked at me like I was nuts because I didn't take all this news in the same way a lot of them did, but honestly, I just couldn't. It was still no big deal for me. I couldn't imagine why the media was giving so much space and air time to the story.

So, I was bought and paid for. Isn't everybody?

The one good thing that came out of this whole deal, at least for me, and some of the others as well, was the fact that I was, for all intent and purposes, no longer an "only child." I think it was Deborah Cupp-Cook of Barberton, who said that finding the group "was like walking down a long, dark hall and finding a light on in a room full of people." I felt as though the people involved in "the Hicks' Babies" scene were my extended family and I think that was the consensus of the whole bunch of us. We all seemed to adopt each other, even to having regular monthly meetings where we would all get together and share both our pain and our pleasure.

As I said before, I liked Jane, and honestly felt a close kinship with her the first time I met her. Her search turned out to be disappointing for her though, and I felt bad about that. She found out that the woman who was most likely her birth mother, a woman named Kitty Goss, had died ten years earlier in a car wreck. I couldn't help but compare the fact that my "parents" had also been killed in a car wreck right after my birth. I had to wonder if that was really true and at the time I wondered then if any of us would ever be able to separate fiction from fact.

In August, 1997, there were sixteen members of the group (nine from Summit County) who decided to make a trip down to Georgia to see what they could find out for themselves. It was strange when I thought about how my life had taken so many strange turns. We had buried Teresa in a small town not too far from McCaysville, and I could not help but consider how ironic it all was: to think that my relatives and my beginnings were in the same area as hers. I don't know if that was another reason I didn't want to go, but it seemed that Georgia was not a top place on my list to visit, since I had left so much pain there the last time.

Another thing too, I was in the middle of my new and booming business and still had little interest in pursuing my beginnings, so I opted out of what I figured might turn out to be a fact-finding mission or a complete disappointment. Besides, I had been involved in some of the publicity stuff which had already been asked of us, like going out to California to be on The Leeza

Gibbons Show. I still did not see the origin of my beginnings, or the manner in which my parents got me, to be any big milestone in my life. The trip to California had, in fact, simply been a neat trip to see a lot of things I would not ordinarily see. Besides, how many times does Leeza ask to have you on her show?

When Jan had called and asked me if I wanted to go with the group to be on the show, I said "Sure, why not?"

By the time the group decided to go to Georgia, one of the adoptees' had found his birth mother who lived in Illinois. He went public with his story on Primetime Live, giving her a bouquet of roses for all the Mother's Days he missed. She told him she was only 22 at the time of his birth, was separated from her husband and didn't have the money to raise him. She also said she had not been allowed by Dr. Hicks to see her baby even once. Unfortunately, the same guy found out that the sister he thought was his birth sister was not that at all, that she had been bought from the Doctor who had lied, saying she was the birth child of the same woman.

The situation was getting extremely painful for some of them, and I found myself wondering why they would put themselves through this kind of agony for someone who was no more than a stranger to them.

In her search, Jane had also met a man who was possibly her half brother. A DNA test did not prove or disprove, but the man insisted Jane looked exactly like his mother, Kitty, and is convinced she is his relative. It was said that a son Kitty also gave up, who would be Jane's brother, had not yet been found. We were told that sibling DNA matches are not as accurate as those run against parents, so it left us with more questions than answers.

One of the women, who was adopted in the 50's, Diane Conrad, talked about how when she was a little girl, her adoptive mother always told her that she was special and had been chosen. She told her that she wanted a little baby so much that she "crossed the border into the big blue hills of Georgia, paid a doctor a handsome amount of money, then hurried back home with the best baby on earth."

So, the group went to Georgia. I stayed in Akron and worked.

The people down in that little Georgia town were of two different persuasions. They either talked their heads off, blabbing about this or that, or they kept their mouths tightly shut. I've often thought if those who didn't say much would speak up, we'd all know a lot more, but some people, especially those who live in that part of the country, often guard their past secrets well, many times taking them to their grave, as old Doctor Hicks did.

Some of the townspeople spoke of the Doctor in glowing terms, saying he was a fine man. Others talked about his "dark side." One woman, Doris Abernathy, resident of McCaysville and local historian, knew Dr. Hicks well. She insisted that the man had some good qualities, but there were a lot of dark things people never knew about him. Another resident, Gene Jones, a retired plumber, told the group he knew Hicks too. He told them the man was an excellent doctor, but that he was money hungry. Others believe he might have even been the father of some of the babies, since there were some whispers of many extramarital affairs he was supposed to have had.

The older people in town also talked in hushed tones about the girls who came there to have their babies. Some said, in those days, and especially in a small southern town, it was a shame to be an unwed mother. Some who found themselves in that predicament would give the baby to a family member rather than allow it to be taken away by strangers. Many have even said they think a large number of the girls were college students who didn't want their parents to find out, or that they were victims of rape or incest and could not bear to have these children in their lives. There were all kinds of theories, opinions, tall tales and faint whispers.

There were no birth records found, but a local antique shop had the registry from the Colonial Hotel where some of the pregnant girls stayed, but there was no way of knowing whether they registered under their real names or not. It was guessed they didn't.

Jane found the trip to Georgia extremely difficult. She and her sister, Michelle Walters, who was also adopted in the same manner, had each other for comfort, but basically a person is by themselves when they make a journey like that, no matter how many people are around.

They said the group went inside the old building that was used by Dr. Hicks. The once-sterile medical rooms were filled with debris from a flood a few years back and had never been cleaned out or occupied again. It was owned by a man named Clark Barker, a retired Air Force Colonel, who gave the group a personal guided tour. It had been used as a health spa, a finance company, a rafting business, and possibly several other things since the Doctor had vacated it. They were told that the original tongue-and-groove knotty pine boards which were in the Doctor's office still covered the walls, and the pink tile was still in the bathrooms. Jane told of standing in the doorway at the back of the red brick clinic where her father had told her she was handed out to him 32 years before. She said her dad also told her he had to put his foot in the door to keep Dr. Hicks from shutting it. He had tried to get more information as well, but that didn't happen.

Another one of the adoptees', Mark Eckenrode, spoke of the story which was told to him by his adoptive parents. He said his mother told him that she had gone into labor in a small town in Georgia while they were traveling through the south. Since he was an only child, he began a genealogy search when he became an adult. He had collected about 600 pages when he discovered the Eckenrodes were not his birth family. At first Mark said he felt some betrayal, but considered it was good that his parents had not had to break the news to him that he was adopted. He figured that saved them the trauma and he felt the whole thing strengthened him. Mark works with homeless men at the Haven of Rest and appears to be quite content with the way his life has turned out. He had wondered about his birth, he said, because his mother never gave him any details and he at times, had almost thought, since he was an only child and born late in his mother's life, that maybe he was not wanted. The discovery, and the trip to Georgia, furnished the birth story that was missing in his life and he said he was glad he went. He is still researching the background of the people who settled in McCaysville, most of whom are of Scotch and Irish descent. Although his adoptive father passed away in 1976, Mark has made it clear to his adoptive mother that finding his biological parents is not his first priority in life. He has said that even if he did find them, it would not be the story of his life, that it would hopefully be just another chapter in a very long book.

I couldn't agree more as far as my own life was concerned. Still, what has happened to many of the "Hicks Babies" is a whole volume of stories, some happy, some sad, and others bittersweet. I can see how much heartache can be caused by a man intent on playing God with people's lives.

Some of the others are still in much pain and anguish. My thoughts on the entire thing is that it is amazing how much a single act or lack of humanity can impact a life, and the lives of so many other people. It was wonderful for those people who could not have children to be able to hold the much wanted baby in their arms, but at what price? And I'm not talking about the measly $1,000 bucks. The cost in pain simply cannot be measured.

Jane related how they all walked through the room where they were told the babies were probably born in. Sadly, she came home with so many more unanswered questions than she went with, as did many of the others.

Edna Spitznas, now McPherson, was one of the women who adopted three children through the clinic, and was the only adoptive parent who went with the group on their journey. Two of her children, Debbie Cupp-Cook and Doreen Addy, were with her. Her son, Dennis, indicated that he had no desire to meet his birth mother. I felt the same way, but now and then, I wonder if perhaps I should have gone along too, not to get answers, but to share this time with the others.

Debbie Cupp-Cook expressed a painful memory of being told by a cousin that she "wasn't really family," because she was adopted. Her life took several bad turns which all seemed to point back to the trauma of feeling different, even though she had two other adopted siblings-from Dr. Hicks as well. Debbie has stated to reporters and others that she feels that years of drinking was simply her way of trying to ease the continual pain, but of course, it did not work. She now has a damaged liver and defective heart, and needs desperately to find the woman who gave her life, to help give her life once again. Her adoptive mother, Edna, was given a letter along with the newborn baby she received at the Hicks clinic.

It said:

"I freely give my daughter to Mr. and Mrs. Charles Spitznas to care for, to clothe and feed in the manner which I cannot. — All my love, Betty Lou Brown."

One night outside a bar, when she was a troubled young girl, Debbie, in a tearful rage, tore the letter into a hundred pieces because she said she felt hopeless and worthless. She did not believe her birth mother wrote the truth, because if she really loved her, Debbie kept thinking, she would have come and found her. Twenty years of drinking took their toll, and even when she managed to get sober and try to get on with her life, she was plagued with health problems. She has chronic pancreatitis, hepatitis C, and a heart abnormality. When she goes to a new doctor, there is always the same question:

"Do any of these problems run in your family?"

She has to tell them she does not know. Like some of the others, she has had some contacts and hopeful encounters, but most have ended in disappointment. After the story broke in May, a man in Tennessee recognized the name Betty Lou Brown. He said it was his mother's name. The woman never came forward for a DNA testing, leaving Debbie in a kind of limbo. She has said that she fluctuates between being totally consumed by it all, and not feeling anything at all. Doctors are suggesting a treatment for her liver that can only be used if her medical history is known. Her prognosis without treatment is, unfortunately, "a slow death."

She is one of the "Hicks Babies" who have been caught up in a terrible dilemma of not knowing what to think, and feeling rejected all over again because the story has been in all the newspapers across the country about her medical need to find her birth mother, yet there has been no response. She cannot believe the woman would not care at all, or come forward to help if she could. She says she has been tempted to take off down south in search of the woman who once gave her life in the hopes she would do it again. Other days, she says she just prays and turns to her adoptive family and her new family, the "Hicks Babies," for comfort and support.

I was told, or I read it in the paper once, that after the group had gone through the clinic down in Georgia, they were all outside, having pictures made and comparing copies of their birth certificates they had picked up at the court house, when somebody came by and asked what was going on.

"What is this...a family reunion?" they asked.

Somebody told them it was.

The Tenth Chapter

Building My Own Empire

"To him nothing is impossible,
who is always dreaming of his past possibilities."
—Carlyle

H ow would you like to become a millionaire?

A billionaire, even?

What would you say if I told you I could make that possible?

You would be skeptical, possibly even arrogant or accusatory, and you might even tell me, in no uncertain terms, what you thought of me and bluntly suggest what I could do with myself.

You would be correct in doing just that.

I can't make anybody a millionaire, or even a half—millionaire. Nobody else can either—except yourself, the lottery, or a rich uncle you haven't offended in some way. The only person who can realistically make you a millionaire is YOU.

What we need to talk about however, is reality.

Reality. That day-to-day stuff we all deal with, or don't deal with.

Did you know that from June of 1997 to June of 1998, there were 1.38 million Americans who filed bankruptcy? Now, being flat broke—with minus finances even—is about as realistic, and about as sad, as you can get. I know. I've been there, done that—and survived.

Did you know that 80 percent of those bankruptcy filings could have been prevented with a mere $200 a month more?

What?

That's it. Not a million a year, not even $50,000 more a year, or $30,000, but a simple $200 a month, which totals up to $2,400 a year. Now, I know that to some people, even that is not exactly pocket change. Still, as a normal individual working person, if you could make that $200 more a month, whether you were in danger of going bankrupt or not, imagine how much your life would improve. It would be like having a bonus every month, money that could be used to catch up on your bills, or simply to enjoy eating out with the kids, a few extra trips to the amusement park or better school clothes.

Let's face it, with only $200 extra money each month, the quality of your life would improve.

It would seem to me that any business or company or individual who offers you a chance to make $200 more a month is much more realistic and, (dare I use the word? Practical,) than those who promise riches beyond your wildest dreams.

I will go so far as saying that you can also become a million-aire, if that's where it's at for you. There's no question about it. If you want it badly enough, and you work long enough, hard enough, and smart enough, you can, in all likelihood, become a millionaire. I did it and I'm certainly no Donald Trump. I'm not above emulating his methods, however. I'm no Anthony Robbins either, but I can certainly listen to his sage advice and implement it wherever it is relevant in my own life and business. I have tapped into the wisdom and experience of Don Lapre, and others like him, to learn everything I can about building my own busi-ness to the point where it is stable enough for me to actually enjoy the fruits of my labors and be able to help others to do the same. There are a lot of ways; honest ways I might add, to become a self-made millionaire, if that's where it's at for you.

I know you've all seen the infomercials where this very young, expensively dressed, guy stands out in front of his beachfront mansion (usually with his exceptionally beautiful blonde wife), or is climbing into his Lear jet, then whisked away in his long white limo, all the while telling you how you too, can become a million-aire—just like him—if you will invest in his almost fool-proof, often guaranteed plan, which will take you from rags to riches in a matter of months, certainly a year or so.

You may also be watching the news when you see him, flanked by his lawyers, being led away to a court house where he is being charged with fraud and misrepresentation of whatever program he is selling. I'm not saying that all of these people you hear claim-ing to show you the "road to riches" are con-men. Many of them have very legitimate and honest systems that can lead to a great deal of money, IF you work hard enough. I'll be the first to admit that it is sometimes—well, almost always—difficult to tell the dif-ference in the con-men and the real deals. The good guys no longer wear white hats and the bad guys aren't always dressed in black with a long cape and a thin black mustache for twirling.

I'll be the first to tell you that I have invested in some of these schemes, out-and-out cons, as well as real opportunities. I've been taken, and I've been involved in some money making deals. Sometimes the actual trial and error method is the only way to find out for sure. I can tell you that a very small percentage of those people who opt to "go for the million," ever get there. Most, unfortunately, are more broke and more disillusioned than ever, once all the cheering has died down and your check has cleared the bank. There are two kinds of people who usually try for those pie-in-the-sky deals, and they are those who are consumed with greed, and those who are absolutely desperate for a better life than what they have. It is the latter category which concerns me. I know from experience that a person who is desperate is probably the easiest mark of all because of the overwhelming need to make things better; not only for himself, but for those he loves and feels as though he has failed them. A desperate man, or woman, will go to almost any lengths to "make things better" for loved-ones and him—or herself. The word "realistic" doesn't even begin to enter into it when you have reached rock bottom; either through circumstances, rotten luck, fate, or your own poor management.

So, when I mention realistic methods to some people, they really don't want to hear it. They want—absolutely have to have!—miracles, not reality. The one thing they fail to realize, however, is that sometimes it is the reality of life that turns out to be the real miracle after all.

Herbalife International was one of the realistic programs which taught me that, when done correctly, there is money to be made in some of the same types of sales. I have, in the past, made a decent living selling their products. It was just that after awhile, I realized that I could implement the other things I had learned, (yes, even from Big Bad Bob) PLUS what I'd gathered from some of the greatest motivational speakers and writers in the world, to build a business that would give me the financial resources and stability I had always wanted and at the same time I could provide some financial relief not only to those who were teetering on the brink of bankruptcy, but also to those who just wanted to improve their lifestyle and that of their family, just enough to make life more pleasant.

I believe money, (or lack of it, which results in a sub-standard way of living,) is not only the cause of some of the major unhappiness in the world. It also causes so much turmoil within families, that there are divorces, child and spousal abuse, wayward children and an overall hopelessness, all because of the lack of resources to "make things better." Now, before I'm called on the carpet by religious leaders saying that the basic cause for man's unhappiness is his separation from God or whatever higher power they choose, and I can appreciate that, however, it was God's original plan in the Garden of Eden that man (and woman) should have it all, that they should live amid beauty and bounty. It was the man and woman who fouled it all up and were banished from the garden to earn their living by the sweat of their brow. This is not a book about getting your act together with your Creator, although that should always be your first priority. The second priority, and one that you are destined to follow is, without a doubt, your ability to earn a living, to strive for the kind of beauty and joy that was the first intention of the Almighty.

Now that we have that settled, let's talk about how to do that—realistically.

What I meant to do from the very first concept of this book was to offer a motivational road map for the ordinary man or woman who is struggling to make those financially starved ends meet. The reason I've offered so much of my personal life is because I wanted to make it clear that I was not born with a silver spoon in my mouth, that I had no "rich uncle," and I certainly have not won the lottery. I wanted to show that I had been down as low as any individual could possibly get—even to the point of checking out on my own—and yet through the love and care of other human beings—or a deep perseverance that came out of strengths I never knew I had, I was able to overcome some of the most awesome obstacles anyone could ever face. There were times when I feel as though I had actually looked into the jaws of death and managed to get away by the skin of my teeth. That's the reason for the title of the book—If I can make it back from where I was, all the way to where I am—Anybody, Anybody Can.

In looking for a place where I began, I found it difficult to pinpoint an exact time and location. I would have to guess that the beginning may have taken place exactly where I did—back in that backwoods clinic, as I was being passed, fresh from the birth canal of some unknown woman, through a small doorway into the arms of strangers who purchased me like any other item.

Who knows how soon memories develop or how soon the strength for survival takes over. It may be more immediate than we ever suspect and there are no scientists, or behavioral study groups who know for sure. It is one of life's great mysteries and I would say that it's just as well. Some things may be better left unknown.

What I do know is that it seemed to me that I was born with a burning desire to accomplish, to achieve, to get from there to here as quickly as possible. That didn't happen, of course. My journey has been rocky, often rough, filled with obstacles and forever treacherous. At the same time, it has been fantastic. Ask me if I'd like to be anybody else but Gary Shawkey and guess what the answer will be.

I like where the journey has brought me, and I want very much to encourage, advise, aid, assist and support those who have traveled this kind of journey as well as those who are only reaching for the low stars. It's an effort worth the time and if it can lead to one single person enjoying only a degree of more happiness, then I will have been even more successful.

Now, people who know me will say right away, "Hey, ol Gary's writing a book to line his pockets a little more, or to advance his business into a higher bracket—He ain't doin' it outta the goodness of his heart"—don't believe that for a minute. To that charge, I answer, "all right, you got me square in the center." It's true that I hope this book will be a success, that it will make a lot of money; that it will be talked about as a helpful as well as an entertaining piece of literature. Guilty, as charged. And, yes, I hope it will advance my business into an even larger entity. Isn't that what every businessman or woman worth their salt wants? In one of his movies, Michael Douglas made the much quoted statement, "Greed is not a dirty word," and maybe in the context of what he was discussing, and maybe it's not, but when it hurts others and takes from others, it is not only a dirty word, it is obscene. However, success is not, and never has been, a dirty word. In fact, any kind of worthwhile accomplishment brings with it not only the monetary rewards, but offers a kind of satisfaction not found in anything else.

I did it.

I built it.

I painted that picture.

I raised that child.

I planted that tree.

I helped that person.

I completed my course.

I did it.

And, I did it well.

Satisfaction is personified in those things. It's the same for me
as it is for you and success is not something anybody should be
ashamed of. I take a lot of pride in knowing that finally—after all
the downs and desperate times—I managed to get my footing on
secure enough ground to make some progress toward the top of
the mountain. I've heard people say the satisfaction comes from
the climbing, not from being at the summit, and I ask them how
they even know when they have reached the summit. I believe
most people climb all their lives and the summit only represents
the end of life. For some, the summit may come very close to the
bottom, while others are much higher up with a much broader
view of the entire universe. I, for one, am still climbing. I think
those who have achieved a certain amount of success, even when
they claim to be retired, are still going forward. I would hope they
have a little more time to enjoy the view they've reached, and
maybe even take time to sit on the plateau and rest a little longer,
but in their own way, still moving onward toward their own personal summit.

Since it is necessary, for the point of this book to go forward, I
have to pick a place to begin with the business I've built over the
last two years. The seed, or the gem of an idea had been planted
long ago, perhaps in Georgia the first time, or the night before
Teresa died. It could have been in Texas, or diving for sea urchins
off the coast of Washington or driving away from a crying child
who had just lost her mother. It could have been while I was in
grade school, or any other time, but the seed was there, and it ger-

minated, coming to the surface sometime, perhaps, in the year 1995, and then taking further shape about January, 1996.

Having worked for Herbalife, as I have said, taught me a lot about business; both mail order and direct selling. With the extensive research I had done, I knew there was a way that I could take what I had learned and improve on it. What I had found in working for some of the companies was that there was an excessive amount of product which had to be purchased from the company in order for the low man on the totem pole to get anywhere. And, if there was a loss, or an inability to move this product, it was the little guy who got stuck with a garage or basement full of multi-colored gizmos which he could not sell. He, or she, of course, was the loser and the company continued on their merry way, making money hand over fist.

Good for the company. Bad for the poor schmuck who was working his butt off and still not getting anywhere. Often, unless he was a super salesman or had an inexhaustible number of willing and financially well-off relatives and friends ready to purchase his wares, he was not even breaking even.

I think the reason I was always able to do well was because I could sell the proverbial ice boxes to Eskimos—or so I'd been told. I had been working in sales for 15 years and most of that time was very successful. It was only shortly before and immediately after Teresa's death that I lost all incentive. My sales had dropped and the checks plummeted. I felt as though I had no base or support for anything, and for most of the time, I didn't even care. I pushed both my children from my mind and wallowed in the worst kind of self-pity. I had earned it, I told myself. I deserved to be miserable and I deserved the chance to wallow in it. I let it consume me for a very long time. Still, I knew, even during those worst times, that if I once again applied myself, I could pull myself out of the pit I found myself in.

For a long time I didn't want to, but with the love and support of my Aunt Gloria, as well as some others who were always there for me, I managed to crawl up from the bottom and try once again to make something of myself. In spite of everything else, I knew I still had Dawn and Joey, and I also knew that this kind of self-pity was not going to support them, nor was it going to be good for them to see their father in the depths of despair.

Then there was Stephanie.

Had I not met Stephanie Coldwell, who knows where I would have ended up? I had honestly believed, when Teresa died, that I would never again be able to give my whole heart to anyone. The pain was too intense, and the agony too much, to allow anyone to get near me again. Even when I met Stephanie, I knew she was a wonderful woman, but I found myself being almost afraid to allow myself to care for anyone, much less love them.

She had seen the Herbalife ad in the paper and called up about being a distributor. She said she was divorced, with two small children and was working in adult foster care with the mentally retarded. She could use the extra money she might make from selling Herbalife; that is, if it worked, which she was going to try before she agreed to sell it.

Good looking women were not new to me; even smart, good looking women had not been all that rare in my life. This one, I knew right from the first, was all that and more. There was an honest quality about her that showed right in her pretty face that was framed by a mass of curly brown hair. Right away I knew she was not the type of woman who could be fooled even by somebody like Big Bad Bob—good as he was with words. She had a way of looking right through you and I began to realize that this was the kind of woman I had needed, not only in my personal life, but in my business as well. She was well-educated and had a lot of common sense to boot. In addition, like me, she had been hurt in her time and knew how to step carefully into whatever situation that presented itself.

I remember sitting at her dining room table and explaining the product to her, telling her what she could expect and not expect. She listened carefully and weighed her decision carefully even before she agreed to try the Herbalife product. Best of all, she became my friend in those first weeks and months. I even came to depend on her, asked her advice and found myself taking it.

Little by little, however, I began to come back to life and interest in my work increased, even though I was becoming more and more disenchanted with the business and how it worked a lot better for the company than the representatives. Of course, that's the way most companies operate that become major successes, but still, I wondered if there was a better way, one which would benefit all concerned in a fairer playing field.

If I could sell their product, I thought, why couldn't I sell my own? Even though I was aware I could move products, I knew there was more that I wanted out of a career, a life. Because I had taken note of these people such as Lapre and Robbins, I focused my abilities toward building something of my own.

Unlike it had been in the early years, when I was repeatedly told that I should "get a real job," Stephanie was completely supportive and very encouraging. She was even the one who encouraged me to send for the Don Lapre "Making Money Package" which would further instruct me in running my own business and further developing my own potential. From the first reading, something clicked. I knew I had finally hit on a winner and that I would be able to finally start making things work. Stephanie continued to believe in me and in my ability to accomplish whatever I set out to do. That was, and is, a big plus in any business: to have somebody you care about, and whose judgment you trust, to believe you can move those mountains at the same time you're climbing them.

It was nothing less than a miracle to me that I found myself falling in love with Stephanie, and even more importantly, she seemed to feel the same way about me. I loved her children and after she met Dawn and Joey, I could tell she had plenty of room in her heart for my children as well.

I had always heard that when the right time for the right person to come into your life will happen, it would. I found this to be true not only from a personal point of view, but from business as well.

Rhonda Tafoya was a friend of Stephanie's. She was also very smart and was a very hard worker. I remember Stephanie telling her to watch out for me, that I would sell her some Herbalife whether she wanted it or not. She just laughed and jumped right into the group, becoming another person who was a very positive influence in my life. She had gone to work for me as I was trying to get my feet back on the ground. She was also in my corner from the beginning, and yes, I think I sold her a bunch of Herbalife products the first time I met her. She also told Stephanie that I was going places, that I would be super successful in a very short time. She claims to have recognized my potential right away, and for that, I thank her profusely. I believe there are two things that can push a person toward the top more than anything else. One is having people who believe you can do the thing you are undertaking, so you'll work twice as hard because you don't want to disappoint them, or let them down. Two, it's having people saying you can't amount to nothing, and are standing back smugly waiting for you to fall off the mountain on your hind end, or your head. You are bound and determined to prove those people wrong, so you can sit upon your higher perch and look down your successful nose at them still struggling around at the bottom.

It's the old "I won't let you down" and the "I'll show 'em" syndromes. Works nearly every time. I, by George, had both incentives.

Several things came together at once to form what was beginning to blossom into the business I was thinking of forming. I began researching more and more products, attending seminars, conventions and reading everything I could get my hands on. I was almost like a runaway train. I was going somewhere—and I was going fast. The only thing I had to do is get behind the wheel and make sure I guided it in the right direction or I would crash and burn as I had done so many times before.

I honestly believe one of the reasons I managed to get this crazy show on the road was the simple premise behind it. I knew that I not only wanted to make it a success, and to make money, but I wanted to take a bunch of people with me. I wanted the company to be where the single Mom in Georgia, the car salesman in Indiana, the housewife in Utah, or the struggling actor in California, could implement my program, manage to make enough money to keep ahead of the bill collectors, and manage to take in a movie)or at least a trip to McDonalds once or twice a week). I wanted to know that my company could be that $200 a month which stood between them and disaster, bankruptcy or complete despondency.

I didn't care who the people were or how much money they had, or didn't have, I wanted it to work for them, and I won't kid you, I wanted it to work for me too. At this point in my life, I knew I had to get it together, once and for all, or lose out on the whole game of life.

The game of life included Stephanie. I was not the kind of person to keep a hard shell around my feelings for the rest of my life and with her ability to show me life was not all bad, I finally admitted that I was head over heels in love, not only with her, but with her two children as well.

After Stephanie and I married, I knew I now had four children to think about, to provide for, and to make sure they were never abandoned the way I had once abandoned Dawn.

It could not happen again. I wouldn't allow it to.

Rhonda, who has a great head for business, and was a single mother in need of a better way of life for her two children and herself, had believed in me and my plans for a business, but at the same time she had a reasonably secure position in the medical field and it was difficult for her to let go of that to come with me. At first, she worked part time, then later, made the ultimate commitment, quit her job and came to work with me in my new company.

We started out with about $400 in cold hard cash. No, not $4,000, $40,000 or $400,000 that would be a more likely the amount it would take to launch any new company. It was $400, and that was all.

I spent about eight months working with other products I believed in before formulating my own product line with my own marketing plan, which was so simple anybody could be successful with it.

In 1997, I launched my own company, "Incredible Products."

And where did I get these Incredible Products?

Same place I got everything else. They were there all along, I just had to go looking for them. First, I asked myself what I wanted to do, what to sell and how to go about it. Because of my years with Herbalife, I knew of the continually growing need for vitamin supplements, health products, weight loss and alternative health care products. It was the coming thing, the "then" thing, because people were becoming very tired of pharmaceutical companies giving them bad medicine and charging them the still painful arm and leg for it.

People wanted good health, but they wanted it naturally, from natural products. People wanted to lose weight, but they had seen first hand what the legitimate medical profession and the illegitimate fat-doctors had done to help them. They wanted more energy. They wanted to feel better, but they were flat-out sick and tired of stuffing chemicals into their bodies. Plain old common sense tells us all those toxic materials can cause toxic effects.

I had a beginning, and from that beginning I did more and more research. I attended a chiropractic convention where I met several chiropractors who enlightened me on several kinds of alternative health care. Since I could not sell chiropractic care through salespeople and through the mail, I decided to study the products they spoke about, trusted; believed in.

I had gone into partnership with a local Chiropractor in Akron who believed in alternative health care and extolled the value of chiropractic care and supplements in place of chemical medicines. Even though our partnership was short—lived, I learned a great deal from him about the benefits of taking care of your own body rather than depending on the medical profession. It wasn't that either of us was totally anti-medicine, but it became apparent that there were a lot of mistakes and mistruths in that field. I learned from him to listen to my own body first, so I could find a better health plan to fit my own lifestyle and needs. I did not always follow what I had learned, but I knew it worked, and from time to time I tried to follow the "eat right, exercise, get adjustments and take supplements rules." When I did, I always felt better.

First, I went to a distributor in Pennsylvania where the product I was interested in was shown to me. They explained its usage, its benefits, its costs, the whole nine-yards, and I began there.

From the beginning, when Stephanie, Rhonda and I opened the small storefront on South Main Street, I had these ground rules for the business:

There will be no $1,000 purchase of products necessary to become one of my representatives.

There will be no way I expect my representatives to stock up a garage full of crap they can't even sell to their relatives and friends who may already be shunning them for fear of having to buy some stuff they neither wanted nor needed. No way did I want Sally Homemaker, who was desperately in debt already and not knowing where her kid's school supplies were coming from; to have to invest a bunch of money she didn't have, into a bunch of doodle she might not even be able to sell.

I also did not want any product to be sold that might earn the representative a thousand dollars a month, then fall to a thousand dollars a year. I wanted something substantial and stable and steady. None of these things, of course, had described what I had been involved with personally, and how I had lived in the past, but somehow everything just seemed to be falling into place— finally.

My product would be a 30-day supply plan so that there would be a steady income for the representative and the company as well. It was a marketing concept geared toward the average person; that person who wanted and/or needed that extra $200 a month or maybe even more. It was really up to him or her.

This plan was not about "selling" or even distributorship, or offering false hopes to those desperate people wanting to have a few extra groceries and a new outfit now and then. I never once offered to make them "millionaires," although if they wanted to establish their own business with this plan in mind, I could assure them it could be done. I felt however, it was more important to pay somebody's light bill than to encourage somebody's dream of yachts and airplanes.

My plan was that they would first be using the product themselves, and it would be working for them. Then, by word of mouth, referrals, as well as through small advertisements, they would hand out samples to those interested in the product. The recipient of the samples would use them and like them, and then when they dialed the 800 number to make the call to order more, they would give the ID number of the representative that was listed on the brochures which came with the sample packets.

The overall plan was to allow that person who worked for Incredible Products to make that $200 a month which would keep them afloat until their life improved from another angle, a better job, a raise, or even an idea for their own business.

Simple. Easy. You betcha.

I was asked how we got people to keep ordering, and the answer was once again, very simple. Give them something that was helpful to them, and something that added value to their lives, either in better health, weight loss, or higher energy, and they would order again and again. Why not?

From the beginning I wanted a product, or products, people would buy anyway, something they needed anyway. I just wanted to be the one who furnished it to them for a reasonable price, through representatives who were also making a reasonable commission. We gave our people free sample packets and free brochures, and we did the advertising. They only had to give away the free samples and wait for the checks to come in.

I began with three products which I believed in myself, which I had tried personally, (and used Stephanie and Rhonda as a guinea pigs as well) and found to be effective. As a personal testimony, I was a walking advertisement for the weight loss product. I once tipped the scales at 340 pounds and through the herbal weight loss product, I lost 53 pounds, and I'm still taking it off at a much slower pace, but it's coming off just the same. At that point, I had no problem extolling the virtues of our product, as I knew other users would not either.

In 1996, I was very pleased to find out at the end of the year that I had grossed $200,000 in product sales. Now, that may not seem like much to some other big company owners, or even small company owners, but I was pleased. I wasn't satisfied, however, because I knew we could do much better if I implemented my own marketing plan and formulated my own product line.

Did that.

At the end of 1997, Incredible Products had grossed more than $4 million in sales. I had had the honor of being inducted into the "International Who's Who of Business Professionals & Entrepreneurs" that same year. I had a nationally known, successful radio show and was regularly showcased in the famous TV show, "Making Money" with Don Lapre, which produced over $75 million in five years. What was even more important to me was the fact that I had been able to give people the tools, strategy and information they needed to get healthy and make that extra money it takes to get along. I ended up with more than 20,000 people that were involved in my program.

Again, I was pleased, although not quite satisfied. In 1998, I began to re-vamp the marketing and manufacture our own products, plus other products which we felt were not only good for the company, but good for our distributors, our representatives, and our customers who had made it possible for us to come this far, this fast.

I don't recall when I realized it, but somewhere along the way I developed, along with my own products, a new philosophy—at least for me it was new—that if you first concentrate on taking care of other people, the good things and the success will just naturally come to you. I know. I know, there are those of you skeptics out there, and there are those of you who may have been treated what you felt was less than fair by me (back when I was still practicing the Bob Fullerton system) who will fall down on the floor laughing at my sudden "good guy" attack, but I'm here to tell you, it works! It's not a new theory at all. In fact, I believe it is not only touted by many of those inspirational and motivational speakers of today, but by an even older volume of recorded words.

Something about 'doing unto others'... I think.

The Eleventh Chapter

Ramblin' Fever . . . Again

"Most men have more courage
than even they themselves think they have."
—Greville

Sometimes, I think my whole life was like one country song after another. In 1998, I began to consider moving again. I think it was Glen Campbell who sang about "an elusive dream," and how the woman in his life might be tired of following it—but did it all the same.

"You went with me to Alabama — and things looked good in Birmingham..." following again, but not finding it there, and having to move on. I came home from work one night and asked Stephanie how she would like to live in Florida. Once more, she surprised me by not reacting the way most women would have. She asked why I thought we should go, and of course she was aware that I had been talking to a company in Florida who expressed an interest in my half of the business.

"What's the deal?" she asked.

"It's great," I replied. "We get a house and a car, and I get a top executive position in the company, plus a great salary and a lot of money for selling them my half of the company." It was, as they say, an offer I could not refuse. I think I also forgot that old chestnut that warns you, "if something sounds too good to be true, it probably is."

It was.

Not right away, however.

We packed up and moved to the sunshine shores of Tampa. Things looked great. Things were in fact, great. Not once did the ugly phrase 'corporate take-over' ever enter my head.

Then, I lost it. Just like that, I lost it. Lost everything. I could have fought the takeover, possibly might have won my case, but it would have cost me more than it would have been worth at that point. So, once again, I found myself back to square one—even further back.

When I had to tell Stephanie the company deal was over, I felt horrible, but once again, she took it in stride. We had to move out of the company house immediately, had to give up the company car on the spot, plus all the perks of being an executive—the generous and steady paycheck included.

Fortunately, we had saved a little money, but once again I went to the borrowing well, getting money from her folks and mine so we could keep going. There was something different about this time, however, that gave me great encouragement. It was the self confidence I had gained while working at my own business. As horrific as the take-over had been, and as much as we had lost, I felt totally confident that we could pull out of the slump and begin again. Still, I gotta be honest, I was scared—but I was not desperate mind you, nor was I so scared that I couldn't think straight.

We started out by driving around through Florida to find a place to live that was not as expensive as Tampa. Only a day or so later, we drove into the little town of Spring Hill, and we both knew before either one of us said a word that this was the place for us to start all over again.

And, it was.

We found a house, moved our stuff and the kids in, and both of us went to work looking for a new business on the Internet. First, we looked for a product to sell, and when we found it, we gave our business a new name, Bodies Best. We found an herbal product called HGH, which stimulated the body's pituitary glands to generate better health. It was, in fact, an excellent product that worked wonders for a lot of people. We headlined our product with "Get Healthy, Wealthy & Wise," followed by the sub-title of "Get Healthy! Get Rich! Here's YOUR home business solution."

We offered to send those who were interested a complete information pack, a free sample of the Weight Loss and Energy Booster and a free Web Site for them to promote. We also promised to work one-on-one with each individual and we charged no fee to join. That way, we were not offering some "big deal," the way some companies do, then abandon them once we got the money in hand. We allowed them to "try it out," to see if it worked before committing themselves to any payment or joining the program. The 30 days we allowed them to try it let them know if they wanted to, or even could, succeed at this business opportunity we were offering them. Of course, they didn't make any bonuses and they could not remain active unless they made a $49.95 retail purchase each month of either product. I mean, hey, we were generous but nothing is free except a chance to see if it works. Since I knew it worked, I felt confident we would get a lot of people signing up for the program.

When you have a great product, what's to stop you from selling? In the beginning, I needed to know first hand if the product worked and as soon as I discovered it did, I had no problem selling it.

One of the people who had also been with me from time to time, through thick and thin, rich and poor, was Rick Fields. Rick is now my best friend and I trust him with my life.

Bodies Best came into being. We set up our website on the Internet to let people know what we had to sell and why they ought to buy it. Stephanie marketed and I sold. She was great at marketing, and if I do say so myself, I was great at selling. Thankfully, we were a good solid team, and in sixty days we knew we were going to be all right. Ninety days passed, we had our debts paid back and were totally self-sufficient.

"You know that just goes to show you that if a person is motivated enough, he can make things work," I said to Stephanie. "People who need to make money for themselves can do it if they believe they can."

She sat there looking at me for a long time before she spoke. She knew how much I admired Tony Robbins and Don Lapre and I guess she wondered why I had not thought of it before. "I think you would make a great motivational speaker, or that you might sell a program telling people how to do what you just did," Stephanie said, still looking directly at me. "You could help a lot of people make money and have a better life, and you could help yourself at the same time. What could be better than that?"

What, indeed?

And, it was true that even in selling, I was motivating people. That's what a motivational speaker or counselor does—sell people on the idea that they can do whatever it is they dream of doing or need to doing at the time.

In this part of my story I have tried to tell you about the obstacles I have had to overcome, sometimes simply to live. Like I said in the beginning of this first book, we needed to get on a personal level. It is my main rule in life. I have made all the mistakes and sometimes made them two or three times. I think perhaps it is sometimes not what you learn to do in life, but what you learn NOT to do. For, if we all went through life without doing any of the stupid, dumb and downright ignorant things, we would reach success a lot sooner than most people.

I can teach you a lot of things—and in the book that follows entitled "Back to Basics," part two of the "Anybody Can..." series already in progress, I will. I will teach you how to make money—sometimes lots of it—sometimes enough to make life a lot more comfortable. I will walk with you step-by-step and even hold your hand if need be.

Following my International Career Opportunities, you will never again be one of those people who is "out of work," a victim of downsizing or company bankruptcies—and even if you were, you would not be "out of the mainstream" long. Getting back up after a hard fall is what I do best—and what I can easily teach. I will offer you money making packages that may not take you to "Easy Street," but you will enjoy "Comfort Avenue" or "Satisfied Lane" a lot more. If starting your own business is where it's at for you, then you are talking to the right person.

I have been called a "marketing guru," whatever that is supposed to mean, but I know what I know and that it works. I have been in the trenches and I have picked the shrapnel pieces out of my hinder-parts. I know how it is done, and I can show you. A lot of people turn the other way when "money over the Internet" is mentioned, thinking it is just another scam or something that will earn you a small profit that is worth less than the trouble it takes to make it.

I would venture to say that as many as 95 percent of the people do not know what to do next. We are living in an uncertain economy, to say the least, and like the smart investors who make sure their portfolio is diversified; you need to do the same with the way you make money. If one thing goes down the tubes, there needs to be ten more things in the works, with at least eight of them working hard for you and bringing in the money. We hear warnings all the time about that "Magic Pill" whether it is to lose weight, or make a million. Well, some people have found something akin to that actual "Magic Pill," and they are making it work for them.

I have one program called ProMoneyMail that has made successful businessmen and women out of thousands of people. I can easily promise you that you will not be a millionaire tomorrow on any of the money making plans I can show you—but you will succeed. I can even guarantee that the average marketer will find a reasonable level of success. Of course, that may not be the big yachts or the mansions or spending your summers in a Villa in the south of France, but it is a beginning—and brother or sister, it ain't bad!

I am not as rich as Bill Gates, or even in the top 500, but I do very well, thank you. I am, by all measures of things that equal success, rich. Primarily rich because I have achieved that which I set out to do—to make a good living for my family and to succeed in doing something I enjoy so much I would almost do it for nothing—fact is, I have done it for nothing, more times than I want to remember. Setting goals is a good thing, but I have never actually sat down and made a list of the things I wanted to do, the places I wanted to go and the money I would like to make in any certain period of time. Oh, I do recall wanting to be a millionaire before I was thirty and I probably made a lot more than that before then— trouble was, I didn't have it. It got lost somewhere along the way. But, I came back, and I succeeded again—and again. I never went from rags to riches, but actually from dead broke to pretty well off, time and time again. I have not only "made it" this time, but kept it made.

I did. You can.

I was, and still am, a perfect example of a person who "can, if they believe they can." Now, this does not mean they can jump off a forty story building without a parachute and land all in one piece—even if they truly believe they can. It doesn't mean they can walk on water or dance over hot coals... or, does it?

Well, let me back up here, maybe they can dance, or certainly walk, on hot coals. I did that, too. I even made the Guinness Book of World Records, shattering the world record for distance by fire walking in Orlando, Florida.

†The Records people were shocked to find that the fire I walked on was hotter than their gauge could measure—heating up to 2,000 degrees. Everyone from Guinness completely freaked out and gave me 3 world records. One, the longest (165 feet), two, the hottest (1,800∞F+), and three, the longest—hottest ever recorded. They even retired the record because it is too dangerous and they do not want to be held responsible for some nut trying to beat me.

Now, before somebody has me declared totally insane, let me explain that some of your best people are avid firewalkers. The famous author, motivator and entrepreneur, Tony Robbins, has been teaching fire walking for several years now, and it is his belief that a person who completes a fire walk can easily say — and mean it: "If I can do this, I can do anything."

As Tony is fond of saying, life itself is a fire walk. God knows, I've certainly walked through hot coals and seemingly through the pits of hell a time or two, but to actually choose to take off your shoes and walk across a bed of hot coals might appear to be fool-hardy, to say the least. It was from Tony that I learned to over-come the fear of walking over hot coals. Like most people, I had the illusion that it was painful, dangerous, and all but impossible. He explained to those of us who came to Orlando back in 1997 to see what this "fire walking" was all about, that the clever ones always win, fanning their inner fears and inner fires in exchange for money. But hey, business is business, and Tony Robbins was not only a fire walker himself, but a great entertainer and a superb life teacher. His International Fire walk Seminars, "Unleash The Power Within," the same name as his best-selling book, have been presented all over the world. It is not a new thing, this fire walk-ing. In fact, the practice of fire walking is quite ancient, the oldest reference to it goes back more than 3,000 years, when ascetics in India walked on embers to test and purify themselves. The Japanese people gather by the tens of thousands every year for several fire walking rituals. The Priests there say it was first held more than 1,300 years ago by "yamabushi," mystics who mix Buddhist beliefs with the nature-worship of Japan's native Shinto.

Tony took advantage of the "New Age" interest in the fire walking popularity in the United States and in Europe, and in the past ten years, hundreds of thousands of people walked over hot coals in the U.S. Worldwide the number rose to two million peo-ple. I was one of those. For some, it is a spiritual, sacred ritual and unfortunately, Tony has been criticized by some for turning it into a fad or a way to make money. But I think it is what you make it — and it is one of the most amazing things you would ever undertake—to be able to know you could succeed in something most people only gasp at when it is mentioned.

In some countries, such as India, Spain, Tibet, Sri Lanka, China Japan, Bali, Fiji as well as several others, fire walking is purely a spiritual practice. The Balinese believe the gods to be "children of the people", so most of the fire walk dances are performed by children. In Hawaii, the Kahunas walk over semi-molten lava, offering deep respect to the goddess, Pele. Many of these cultures know that fire is a sacred element of nature, and of life itself. To many it is a deeply spiritual experience that uplifts, rejuvenates, renews, and heals the inner fires. Physicists have studied fire walking since the 1930s and have concluded that it is easily explained and is actually easily done. The bed of coals is composed of burning embers that are spread rather thin. The temperature is usually from around 450 to 1000 degrees hot, and the ashes covering the coals are poor transmitters of heat. They say this is why a person can tolerate a brief walk across the coals without fear of serious burns. One of the people who studied it, advised those people who were considering the walk, however, "take brisk light steps, with toes curled upwards, and don't hang around."

I agree. You do not want to wait for a bus standing on the hot coals.

One thing I want to make clear here too, is that not everybody who thinks they can fire walk—can. Not everybody who holds a seminar to teach fire walking—can, either. In October, 2001, a group of about 100 people from marketing at Burger King in Miami, Florida hired a consultant to do some team building, including a fire walk. About a dozen or so participants received first and second degree burns.

So, those people who criticize Tony for "making money" at his fire walking seminars, do not realize that he does not take the practice lightly. He is a veteran and a master firewalker with more than 20 years experience. Peggy Dylan and Tolly Burkan began instructing fire walking based on the Tibetan Buddhist model, and are the people responsible for introducing fire walking to today's world. In fact, Tolly is the man who trained Tony twenty years ago, and Tony is the man who taught me. Since that time I have held several fire walking seminars of my own, and it is amazing how people who choose to walk over these hot coals come out with the feeling that "they can do anything." Tony still has the best record for "turning fear into power."

One of the first things people say to me when they hear about the "fire walking," is "What's the matter, are you crazy?" Many of those people who come to my seminars come out of curiosity, without any intention whatsoever of stepping out onto that bed of hot coals. I can almost guarantee that out of 100 people in a group—by the time I am finished talking to them—95, or maybe even 98 of them, will actually take the steps and complete the practice. The amazement and actual surprise at their own abilities and courage, exhibited upon completing such a feat is almost as miraculous as the walk itself. They are changed people, I guarantee that, too!

Don't think so?

Come to one of my B.L.A.S.S.T. Seminars. (Building Leadership and Super Success Training)

So, this is just one of the things I do, yet all of the things I do, add up to the sum total of what I am; what I've become. I started out life in a small clinic in Georgia, sold to an Ohio couple for a fist full of dollars. I have searched most of my life for that elusive dream that has escaped me time and again. I have almost grabbed the brass ring on the Merry-go-round only to fall off my horse and eat the dust of the midway until I could pull myself together again and get back on the golden palomino.

I have not done what I've done alone. There have been so many people who have either guided me, made it possible for me to take some of the less-traveled roads I took, or simply spoke a few words of encouragement when I needed them most. There have been others who have tried like the devil (and him, too) to keep me from making it to the top of the mountain that I was so anxious to reach, just so I could look down on the other side. There are always other mountains to climb, however, other roads to take and other people who will either choose to go with me, or opt to stay behind. There are still some who try to prevent me from moving on to greater realms and completing my journey, but too much has happened to me to allow anyone to tell me I do not have either the confidence, the courage or the raw ability to achieve my goals and dreams.

If there is one thing I want to do—and I think I do—is to infuse others with this confidence and self-assurance that it has taken me years to attain. I do not want everyone—or anyone, for that matter—to have to go through the things I have gone through in order to become successful. I want you to be able to ride a ways on my coat-tails and benefit from my mistakes and my woes, so you can reach those dreams you have always had without having to pay such an exorbitant price for them. I am here for you and have assembled the "Best of the Best" to help anybody willing to take the next step. What is your next step? It's called, "Back to Basics". Send me an Email and let's do this thing together, my friend. anybodycan@garyshawkey.com.

Hey, if I can—Lord knows, ANYBODY CAN!

Epilogue

Here I sit, working at my computer from the comfort of my home office in Florida, and life is good. Exceptionally good, in fact. From my wonderful, loving wife Stephanie and children, to the outstanding team of professionals who are helping me take my network of companies to exciting new levels of success, I'm working with people I both respect and enjoy.

It's a new year now, and everything is fresh and exciting. i'm extremely happy to have this opportunity to share my enthusiasm with you. My new infomercial has been filmed, tested, edited, tested again, and has been viewed throughout the world via the Internet. challenging as well as fun, it was an exciting project all around, and I'm sure once you see it, you'll enjoy it as well.

What an eventful year 2002 was for me and my network of companies! We've been able to lay the groundwork for the worldwide rollout of my master plan and at this very moment, we're preparing the release of BizOppX, our website Portal. BizOppX will provide business tools and personalized training never seen before to anyone seeking to improve their lives through our first-class business opportunities, or even one of their own.

In my deepest heart of hearts, I believe we have the best combination of Internet-based companies to provide each and every person the success they desire. I'm absolutely certain you'll agree after you've seen the totally unique combination I've put together, and if that has your curiosity aroused, you can review all of my companies at www.BizOppXtreme.com any time you wish.

Thank you for taking the time to get to know me through this book. You've had a chance to get a pretty intimate understanding of who I am and what I'm about. Now that you know me, it's my turn to get to know you.

With the infomercial completed, I now have time to do the work I love most: visiting with people such as yourself at my Building Leadership And Super Success Training (B.L.A.S.S.T.) Seminars. Through my personal results coaching and fire walk training, we can create a personal bond that will virtually assure your success in whatever you choose. Join me at the next seminar closest to your area. your life will never be the same again!

In 2003, I'll be training 6,250 Master Coaches, beginning with my "BLASST to Success in 2003" Seminar in San Jose, California. After that, it's on to Brisbane, Australia and London, England with a few hand-picked Master Diamond Coaches, where I'll be training the rest of the Master Coach candidates to ensure people throughout the world will have access to the utmost training and coaching from a truly world-wide group of Master Coaches.

None of these pursuits would be worthwhile if they didn't allow me to achieve my ultimate goal—benefitting the children of the world. Children and their families who are truly in need of assistance will be able to find it through BizOpp 4 Kids and Coaches 4 Kids, my two programs designed to make a difference in the lives of children everywhere. Kids of all ages will be attending life-changing activities that'll set them on the path to success for the rest of their lives at my soon-to-be-finished retreat in the Ohio countryside!

My next book, "Back to Basics," will be finished up here pretty soon, so your next step is to get this book and begin learning what it takes to get started on the Internet toward achieving your own financial independence. Look for the books' release announcement at www.GaryShawkey.com! Join with me and we'll have one heck of a ride!

Cheers! ...and Live to be Outstanding!

Gary Shawkey
Somewhere in Florida—January, 2003